Martin Laurie

Cupids
WAR

THE TRUE STORY OF A HORSE
THAT WENT TO WAR

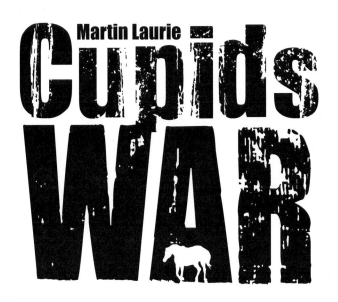

Martin Laurie

Cupids WAR

THE TRUE STORY OF A HORSE
THAT WENT TO WAR

MEREO
Cirencester

Mereo Books

1A The Wool Market Dyer Street Cirencester Gloucestershire GL7 2PR
An imprint of Memoirs Publishing www.mereobooks.com

Cupid's war: 978-1-86151-262-8

First published in Great Britain in 2014
by Mereo Books, an imprint of Memoirs Publishing

The address for Memoirs Publishing Group Limited can be found at
www.memoirspublishing.com

The Memoirs Publishing Group Ltd Reg. No. 7834348

The Memoirs Publishing Group supports both The Forest Stewardship Council® (FSC®) and
the PEFC® leading international forest-certification organisations. Our books carrying both the
FSC label and the PEFC® and are printed on FSC®-certified paper. FSC® is the only
forest-certification scheme supported by the leading environmental organisations including
Greenpeace. Our paper procurement policy can be found at
www.memoirspublishing.com/environment

Cover design - Ray Lipscombe

Typeset in 12/18pt Plantin
by Wiltshire Associates Publisher Services Ltd.

Printed and bound in Great Britain by
Marston Book Services Limited, Oxfordshire

INTRODUCTION

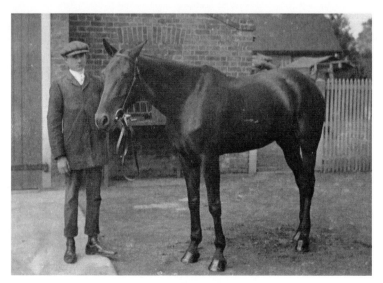

Cupid in 1914

Cupid was a real horse and Vernon, the boy who rode her, was equally real; in fact he was my grandfather.

The first I heard of Cupid was some forty years ago; I was given a book for my birthday and told about the little horse on the same day, because, as I was told, she had made the same journey.

The book was called Romford to Beirut, and it was compiled by Edwin Blackwell and Edwin C. Axe and published by R.W. Humphris, Clacton-on-Sea, on behalf of the old 'B' Battery 271st Brigade R.F.A. It was given to me by my grandfather, who served in 'C' Battery in the same Brigade.

I must confess that on receiving the book as a birthday present all those years ago, I wasn't much interested in it. After I had flicked through it and, I hope, written a suitable letter of thanks, it was abandoned, but fortunately it was not lost.

Many years later I discovered a bundle of First World War letters and on reading them I was reminded of the book and the story of the horse.

The story begins one hundred years ago on 5th August 1914, the day after war was declared. On 17th November 2015 it will be a hundred years since Cupid left these shores, embarking on her long and sometimes arduous journey. She was one of hundreds of thousands, in fact millions, of horses from both sides that went to war, and although Cupid's story is perhaps no more remarkable than many, I thought that as we approach this extraordinary anniversary, it would be interesting to record it before it is lost in the ravages of time.

I am not an historian and have no pretence of being one; I have therefore tried to tell the story from Cupid's point of view. It is a true story, told with a certain amount of artistic licence, and taken entirely from family papers, photographs, letters and the aforementioned book. The story travels from Essex to Beirut via France, Egypt and Palestine.

The story is not intended to cause offence to anybody; much of it is about a part of the world that is still much troubled a century later.

Please enjoy my story, but at the same time remember all those who gave their lives regardless of whose side they fought for during the four long years of the First World War and give some thought also to the horses, without whose courage, loyalty and hard work I think it is reasonable to suggest that the war could not have been fought.

Cupid and Polly

Polly in 1911

Loading horses onto a train, England 1914

Horse lines

Horse teams crossing the desert

Cupid wearing her 'fly fringe'

Flashlight at the water trough

Bosche, the dog that followed Vernon home

Lordy the goose

Cupid's Battery by the Pyramids, April 1916

The foal born in March 1916

CHAPTER ONE

The morning of 16th November 1915 was cold, grey and miserable. It had rained for most of the night and showed no sign of letting up; it was half light and looked like being one of those November days when it really wouldn't get much lighter. The wind howled around the corners of the warehouses and whistled through the gantries of the cranes on the dockside.

These were Southampton docks, and the long train that had arrived at dawn after travelling overnight from Thetford in Norfolk carrying the horses that belonged to a Brigade of Field Artillery was about to be unloaded. Several hundred horses had travelled overnight in what had once been cattle trucks, but since the beginning of the war had been used for nothing other than ferrying horses to the dockside. Southampton was their port of embarkation and they were on their way to the muddy, squalid horrors of the Western Front.

In one of these trucks was Cupid, a pretty five-year-old bay mare, and as the sliding door of the truck was opened she felt the rush of the cold air flooding in, and it made her shiver.

Slowly the horses were led from the train. When Cupid's turn came, the wooden ramp which was used to lead the horses down from the truck, which had once been covered with coconut matting to provide some sort of grip, was in such a slimy state that it was almost impossible for a horse to pass over it and remain upright. Some had shied at it, some had tried to jump over it; each horse was led by two men, one either side to steady their perilous descent. Cupid managed by chance to stay upright and soon found herself standing with her companions tied to a rail in what had been, at the beginning of the war, hastily erected and temporary horse lines which now showed signs of the wear and tear caused by the many thousands of horses that had passed through them in the first fifteen months of the war.

After the long journey in the stifling heat of the cramped and badly-ventilated wagon, where the steam and stench of the horse dung hung heavily in the damp air, the chill of this November morning made the horses hunch. They were stiff from lack of movement and the only shelter was the flapping canvas of the walls and roof of the so called horse lines.

Not only was it perishing cold, it was frightening. The unfamiliar noises from the ship's sirens and the swarming flocks of screeching seagulls that landed all about them, scavenging for any scrap of food and fighting each other over the freshly-laid horse droppings for any morsel that could be found, were very disconcerting.

There were men everywhere, shouting, running, marching. Hundreds of soldiers were stacking kit-bags on the dockside. Others were manhandling the guns, ammunition wagons, forage wagons and all manner of other equipment required by a brigade of artillery. All of this was being made ready to be winched aboard one of the ships. The dockers would argue with the soldiers, and the ship's crew would argue with the dockers, and all the time the rain lashed down in torrents. The whole place stank of coal smoke from the trains, and the ships, and the chimneys of the fires that heated the offices on the quayside. The smoke swirled in the damp air, and everything seemed to be the same cold grey colour.

At last the horses were watered and fed. It was now over twelve hours since they had last been watered, and although the water was foul and black with coal dust, they relished every last drop of it.

Cupid had been with the Brigade since the day after war had been declared on 4th August 1914, and the last fifteen months had changed her life beyond all description.

Cupid was a hunter, a lightweight, standing at about fifteen hands high. She had been born in 1909 and bought in 1911 as a fifteenth birthday present for a boy called Vernon. Both she and Vernon loved hunting and she had had three idyllic years in the Essex countryside. The flat grasslands which still covered much of south Essex in those happy days before the war were ideal for her. The country was dotted with huge elm trees now long gone, and the fields on the home farm where she lived grew the sweetest grass during the long summer months. Life for Cupid was perfect.

Vernon's father, who had bought Cupid for his son in 1911, commanded the local Territorial Field Artillery Battery. On the day that war was declared, the Battery had been mobilised and become part of the Brigade that now languished on the dockside at Southampton. On the day of mobilisation all the horses, bar one, from Cupid's stable were press-ganged into the Battery; namely, Cupid, Flashlight, Nimrod and Polly, also one of the carriage horses. Frolic, the only horse to be left behind, was old and not very sound, otherwise she too no doubt would have been called up.

One of Vernon's father's first duties on mobilisation was to buy horses for the Battery, and on 22nd August 1914 he wrote home:

I have, since the declaration of war, been working 15 to 18 hours a day.

On the day of mobilization I was ordered to buy 131 horses for my Battery, which I did between mid-day on the Wednesday & 11 a.m. on the Sunday, very good horses too I bought, they are all standing in the lines beside me now as I sit writing on my forage wagon, all hogged and trimmed & looking like regular Battery's horses.

On the Sunday we had to harness up & hook in our new horses & march to our war station 17 miles away, all done up to time. I have all my hunters here and one of the carriage horses.

Not long afterwards Vernon, who was now eighteen, had also joined the Battery; he and Cupid were now together again, which was a relief to them both as they settled into their new disciplined lives. Cupid and Polly were from now on to be Vernon's personal horses.

The first few months of the war were spent at a place called Abberton, just south of Colchester, where both men and horses lived under canvas until the weather deteriorated and then, as the days shortened and the bitter east winds howled their way across the North Sea, farm buildings, cottages, and any other available roof space was requisitioned by the military. Many of these places are now lost beneath the deep waters of the reservoir built in the 1930s.

On the day of mobilisation, the men of this Territorial Brigade, who had been part time soldiers, training at weekends and going on summer camp each year, suddenly found themselves full-time soldiers. They had had to leave their civilian jobs and their wives, mothers and families.

Many of them had been farm labourers or ploughmen, some had worked on the railway others as draymen or in factories, and adjusting to their new life was not easy. Fortunately many of these men had at one time worked with horses, and because horses were the mainstay of army life, man and beast had to know each other and work well together, and it wasn't long before a strong bond was built up between them.

On 22nd December 1914, Vernon wrote:

We are billeted in a small cottage and the horses are in two stables about ½ mile apart. It has rained almost every day since I have been here and so the place is rather muddy! But it is ripping to have all these horses and several of our own amongst them, we have a good mixture of horses and men. One splendid man, an ex sailor, awful rough chap who has annexed two horses to look after, both of them frightful kickers, but good workers. He always collects all the bread over from meals and gives it to his horses. Another man has 2 beautiful roans & almost sleeps with them. Nearly all the men are careful and fond of their horses now. One gets a nice variety to ride and I have had some great cross-country rides.

Like the men, the horses had come from all walks of life. Some, like Cupid and her companions, had been hunters. Others had been carriage horses, some had come straight from farms and others had pulled brewery drays or milk floats, and this new disciplined life was difficult for them. The carriage horses and dray horses were not used to pulling guns and ammunition wagons, and they had to work as a team. The military saddles didn't fit properly and were uncomfortable, the harness used by the army was different and hard to get used to, and the schooling for all of them was monotonous and hard work.

Keeping a Brigade of artillery mobile was in itself a full time job; there were farriers and blacksmiths, saddlers and harness makers, wheelwrights and carpenters, all of whom worked tirelessly day and night to keep everything in working order, for this was a Territorial Brigade, and unlike the regular army their equipment was old, second hand, out of date and not up to the hard work put upon it by active service. Most importantly, the Brigade relied on fit and healthy horses, because without them it could go nowhere.

During the last two months of 1914 the Brigade was deployed on the Essex coast; a German invasion was very much expected and many long, cold nights were spent on the foreshore of Mersea Island and other such places waiting for dawn to break, with orders to open fire on any German warships or submarines that might be seen, and that could be heralding the invasion. They would watch and wait in silence in the perishing cold, listening to the waves breaking, and in the early hours great skeins of geese would fly over, as well as thousands of duck heading for their morning feed.

When daylight finally came, only British warships could be seen patrolling the grey waters and never a shot did they fire. The invasion never came, and the remainder of the winter of 1914/1915 was spent monotonously on or around the Essex coast.

The horses needed to be kept fit. Fortunately for Cupid and Vernon, one of the best ways of keeping a horse fit was to go hunting, so as many days as possible were spent doing what they loved most. Commanding officers encouraged the men to go hunting; it improved their horsemanship, steadied their nerve and was very good for the horses.

Eventually some of the ancient and worn-out pre-war equipment was replaced and life began to be more efficient; the men and horses became more used to their new way of life.

At last the spring arrived and Cupid relished the sun on her back and the occasional feed of fresh green grass; also, she was reunited with her old friends Nimrod, Flashlight and Polly. They had been separated during the winter and it was reassuring for her to be with them again.

All the horses were much calmer now; they were very fit and much more used to the discipline and routine of their new life.

One of the most testing and frightening parts of their training had been their first visit to the firing ranges on the coast. The roar of the guns and the screech of the shells whistling through the air had been terrifying, and the stench of the burnt cordite that filled their nostrils and stung their eyes took a good while to become used to. Luckily for Cupid, when she was first taken to the ranges it was Vernon who had taken her, and they trusted each other.

In May 1915, Cupid had her first experience of a long railway journey. The Brigade left Colchester for St Albans, where the Division of which it was part was concentrated; there was a rumour in the air that they were about to be sent abroad. This first train journey, unlike the one that she had just undertaken on that cold November night, had in fact started out quite pleasant; it was summer, the weather was warm and the sun shone. The railway trucks were open-topped, so the air stayed fresh as they rattled through the pretty countryside. But as the night gathered in so did the clouds, the great black clouds of a summer storm.

Some time around midnight the rain began and was soon torrential. Everything was soaked, horses, men and equipment. By the time they reached their destination, Boxmoor Station near Hemel Hempstead, the horses were cold and steaming and the men bad-tempered. It took an age to unload the train. The horses were first; they were led into the station yard, where the men rubbed them down with straw, to help regain their circulation while they waited patiently for the guns and other equipment to come lumbering off the train.

When they finally moved off to their new camp at Gadebridge Park, about a mile north of Hemel Hempstead, the lanes and tracks had become a quagmire and the guns and the wagons became stuck up to their axels in the mud and had to be abandoned until the morning. The men became bad-tempered and the horses struggled to cope.

Cupid, Flashlight, Nimrod and Polly arrived bedraggled at their horse lines at nine o'clock in the morning and at last were fed and watered. The storm had passed and the sun thankfully shone again.

The tired men were desperately trying to make some order from the chaos that had resulted from the storm, and the guns and the rest of the abandoned equipment were finally dragged into the camp. Officers were giving orders, NCOs were shouting and the horses were now being formed up into lines. Row upon row of horses were lined up and tied to ropes strung between stakes. They had been hastily groomed and made to look presentable, but they were unsettled and too close together and had started to become irritable with each other. Some kicked out at their neighbours, some kicked out at the men. One of the lines broke and several horses bolted; confusion reigned, and it was some time before order was at last restored.

Cupid and her friends were standing near each other when a very smelly motorbus, its engine belching black, oily smoke, appeared at the horse lines. The bus had attempted to negotiate the same route up to the camp as the Brigade had taken during the night, but it had become completely stuck in the deep mud, eventually being pulled out and dragged the rest of the way by a team of gun horses. It was only the last hundred yards or so that it had made under its own steam. It was filthy dirty and the red-faced driver was ordered to remove it and get it cleaned. One or two of these new-fangled machines were beginning to appear among units of the Territorial Army and they were not universally popular with the men. They were smelly and always breaking down, and the unfortunate drivers and the mechanics who looked after them were the butt of many jokes.

The dozen or so men who disembarked from the bus were from the Divisional Artillery Veterinary Section, and were there to inspect all the horses to make sure they were fit enough for active service; this would take the rest of the day. When they had finished, several horses were led away, either consigned to the knackers yard or, if they were lucky, returned to civilian life. Mercifully, Cupid, Nimrod, Flashlight and Polly passed out fit for duty.

Three months passed at St Albans, during which time the Brigade were re-armed with new 18-pounder guns. This involved two more journeys by train to Salisbury Plain and back, to practise with their new guns on the Plain.

The rumours continued that they were about to go abroad, but still they remained at St Albans. Eventually at the end of August one more railway journey took them to Thetford, in Norfolk, where they would remain, under canvas in deteriorating weather, until the journey that had brought them here to Southampton on that miserable November morning.

CHAPTER TWO

They watched as the equipment was slowly and painstakingly winched aboard the grey and rusting ship until eventually the horses began to be led one by one up the gangway and into the dark and unfamiliar hold.

This took hours; many of the horses, already unsettled by the events of the morning were unwilling to be led up the gangway and into the foreboding black hole in the side of the ship. It would sometimes take as many as four men to persuade a horse to go up the gangway and commit to the unknown.

Cupid was one of the last to go. She had watched Polly go up the ramp and into the darkness and she followed reasonably calmly. As she reached the top of the gangway, she met Polly coming out again. The soldier who was leading her pulled up sharply and started to remonstrate with the soldier who was leading Polly. There was a lot of arm waving and pointing and then the shouting began again. There was shouting from inside the ship, shouting from the deck of the ship, shouting from the dockside. Eventually an officer with a megaphone started to bellow orders. He was on the dockside and standing on the top of a stepladder, looking rather ridiculous.

Eventually Polly was led back down the gangway and after some difficulty, Cupid was turned around at the top and led back down to rejoin the others at the horse lines. They watched in amazement as one by one all the horses were brought back from the ship.

Due to an error at the embarkation office the whole lot of them had been loaded on to the wrong ship. This unnecessary and frankly exhausting operation had taken the whole day and it was seven o'clock that night, in the pitch dark, when the horses were finally fed and watered again.

Later that night, a man carrying a lantern walked down to the horse lines. He stopped now and again to stroke a horse, adjust or re-tie a piece of flapping canvas that had come adrift. The wind was cold but at last it had stopped raining.

Eventually he found Cupid. It was Vernon; he was off duty, longing for the sleep that hadn't come when he had finally got to his cold camp bed, so he had pulled on his boots, wrapped himself in his British Warm coat, pushed his hat down over his ears and wandered off down to the horse lines.

The smell of the small briar pipe he was smoking reminded Cupid of home and she let out a gentle whinny. He stroked her nose, gently pulled her ears and whispered to her, and this seemed to comfort them both.

Before light the next morning, the whole place was abuzz again. Morning stables were hastily completed, the horses fed and watered and then saddled up by the men.

Soon a long column of horses were waiting at the gates of the dockyard. There was a murmur of conversation from the men on their backs; this was the men talking to their horses, not to each other.

Cupid loved to hear Vernon's gentle voice. It calmed her and settled her. She would do anything for him; they had known each other for so long, each anticipating the other's next move.

The dockyard gates were swung open by the sentries, and the long column flowed out through the gates and onto the streets of Southampton. They clattered through the streets as the local residents were beginning to go about their business, mainly women and children and older men; the young men had all joined Kitchener's Army.

The children were bringing in the coal to help their mothers before going off to school. The milkman, a man of about sixty, hastily pushed his two-wheeled float out of the way, and the enamel jugs clanked together as it mounted the pavement. The post boy on his bicycle tried to keep up with the horses. He was sixteen and longing to be a soldier; his father and brother were already in France, but he had yet to hear of or understand the horrors that were the Western Front.

It was not long before they were out in the country. Cupid had not been ridden since being loaded onto the train at Thetford and at first she was stiff from all the hanging about, but as she started to trot on, the cold left her and she felt free again.

As the light came they entered the New Forest. It was a cold grey dawn, but at least it was dry. For an hour and a half Cupid and Vernon rode through the forest, seeing deer and ponies and flushing pheasants from the bracken. What a joy! They galloped on and jumped a fallen tree. Vernon even let out a loud 'halloa!' when an old dog fox was disturbed from his morning rounds; there were of course no hounds, but the excitement of this early morning ride exhilarated both Cupid and Vernon so much that they forgot the troubles of the previous day and night and were larking about. Cupid's ears were pricked and a wonderful sense of freedom surged through her.

Vernon in this moment of exhilaration forgot that he was a soldier. He forgot just for those few short minutes that he was in the army; he and Cupid were doing what they had done so many times before – riding cross-country without a care in the world.

The real world came crashing back to them when Vernon was reminded in no uncertain terms of his military duties and responsibilities, and the ride back to the docks was not such a happy one.

As they returned to the dockyard, they could see that the equipment was again being loaded onto a ship, an even bigger ship than the one that had caused yesterday's confusion. By midday the horses were being loaded and eventually Cupid was led up the gangway and in through the inky black void.

Being inside the ship was an experience unlike any other during Cupid's life. She only wished that the Vernon was with her, but he was busy with the men, more busy than many of the others in fact; the extra duties that he had been given after the morning's little escapade were going to keep him occupied for most of the night.

Cupid stood amongst the other horses frightened and nervous. Steam was rising from the wooden floor of the horse deck, which had recently been scrubbed and disinfected by the ship's crew; that was their job during the return journey across the Channel.

The ship had plied its way back and forth so many times now, carrying thousands of horses, men and military equipment to the front, that the decking was becoming worn from the endless tramp of the horse's hooves.

The air stank of the disinfectant and the only light was from oil lamps, hung few and far between above their heads, which produced nothing more than a dull glow. The echoing noises were horrendous, the booming and banging was continuous and there was no comforting food or water.

When the last of the horses had been loaded and the gangway removed, the huge iron door was winched shut with an almighty clang. This prevented any further ventilation and the air soon became stale and the temperature rose. The boilers were being stoked in the engine room to build up a head of steam for their departure.

Cupid calmed herself by remembering that short moment of pleasure she had had in the morning. This took her mind back to the days of freedom and hunting. The smell of disinfectant reminded her of her stable at home; there was always a slight smell of disinfectant in the air when she returned from hunting, when she was led into the warm stable with a thick straw bed, and she would wait patiently for her feed.

She could smell the boiling linseed bubbling on the range in the saddle-room, hear the fire crackling in its grate and the man who worked in the stables talking with Vernon about the day as they prepared her feed; then at last it came, bran mash mixed with the hot linseed – what heaven!

Suddenly she felt movement, an alarming swaying movement and then a fearsome judder as the great steam engines began to turn the propellers and the ship eased its way out into the Solent. This was hell, and she feared for her life.

It must be said that for once the horses were probably more comfortable than the men, who were on the open deck where there was no shelter. They huddled together, talking, smoking and reminiscing, and wondering what the future held for them; it was a perishing cold night.

The North-Western Miller had set sail from Southampton at 5 pm on November 17th 1915 and for the majority of the men and horses it would be the last time they saw England for more than three years. Many alas, were destined never to return.

CHAPTER THREE

It was a mercifully calm crossing, but by the time they reached Le Havre in the early hours of the morning of the 18th November, the horses were disorientated and very unsettled. Although the sea had been calm, the continuous rolling of the ship had been nauseating (if that is a feeling that a horse can have); and they were again craving water.

At the same time the men on the open deck were shivering, coughing and grumbling. There had been one brew of tea during the night, but by the time it reached the men it was just lukewarm. None of them had slept and their morale was low when they first saw the faint glow of the lights in the harbour.

It was misty so the lights came and went, and the occasional foghorn sounded, which created a gloomy and forbidding atmosphere. The horses could also hear the faint booming of the foghorns; for them they could have been entering Hades itself.

Eventually the ship was berthed and disembarkation began at about seven o'clock. Again the shouting started, this time in a strange language. The French dockworkers were as bad-tempered as the men on the ship and any order or request was lost in translation. However, eventually the officers and NCOs restored some sort of discipline, and at last the horses were brought out into the fresh air.

Their legs were trembling as they were led down the gangway; some could hardly stagger. There were men waiting at the bottom of the ramp to lead the horses away to be watered; and then each horse was given a nosebag, which contained a very measly amount of food.

As soon as the horses were settled, as much as they could be, the men formed a queue which led into a vast warehouse which had been turned into a sort of gigantic soup kitchen where at last they too were fed.

As daylight slowly gathered on that gloomy Le Havre morning, the men who had been fed first returned to the horse lines and each man leading two horses led them away to the nearby shunting yard, where yet again they were loaded onto a train.

Finally at about six in the evening, both men and horses were aboard the train, which was filthy, damp and cold. The men and horses occupied the same type of wagon; just bare, damp, wooden boards on the floor, not even a layer of straw for the wretched, tired men to sit on and at least attempt some much-needed sleep.

The train rattled slowly through the French countryside for nineteen hours, again with no food or water for either man or beast. The journey was miserable; it was bitterly cold, and raining torrents.

They arrived eventually at St Omer at about three in the morning, where at last they were detrained; the mood amongst the men and horses by this time was that of despair. Both were hungry, thirsty, and exhausted. The men had had little or no sleep since leaving Southampton and the horses were stiff and unwilling.

The yard into which they were unloaded might once have offered some sort of hard standing, but through overuse and weeks of continuous rain, it had turned into a quagmire of thick black mud. There were water troughs at one end to which the horses were led through mud hock deep, but there were so many horses that the men working the two-handled pump could not keep up the supply and it took ages to water all of them.

After they were watered they were again given a very short ration of feed in a nosebag before finally being saddled up. The gun and wagon horses were hooked in and eventually the Brigade was ready to move out. By this time everything was caked in mud and soaking wet. The whole operation had been carried out in the dark and much of the smaller equipment had been lost, dropped and then trodden into the mud by the men and horses.

At last Vernon appeared, carrying his saddlebags over his shoulder and a blanket roll. He attached the bags to either side of Cupid's saddle and the blanket roll at the front over the pommel, and then from his pocket he produced a small peppermint sweet which he fed to Cupid before kissing her on the nose and stroking her ears; he then stiffly climbed into the saddle. Then Polly, ridden by another man, came up alongside them and a slight sense of normality returned.

Slowly the Brigade crept out of St Omer and at last met the main road. Although the surface was ruined, it was at least hard, and relatively free from mud. A faint patch of light appeared in the eastern sky, which reflected in the huge water-filled potholes. The rain had eased to a freezing drizzle and the horses and men were pleased to be moving at last.

In front of them was a journey of about twelve miles and as daylight finally broke Cupid looked about her at the deserted waterlogged countryside. There were a few farmsteads dotted about, one or two with a wisp of smoke coming from the chimney, but most were deserted; there were no animals to be seen, no cattle, no sheep and certainly no horses. There were very few trees and no hedgerows, just a few pollard willows and the odd poplar tree. Most of the trees had been scavenged by troops and the few remaining locals for fuel.

What was this terrible place and why was she here?

On 20th November 1915 they arrived at a place called Lynde. The road had now become so completely churned up by the heavy military traffic that the wheels and springs on the wagons and gun carriages were breaking and progress was slower than ever. Polly was beginning to go lame. She had cast a shoe in the mud, and the man who was riding her had dismounted and was now leading her, ankle deep, through the mud.

When at last they arrived at their billets it was with a huge sense of relief. The billets were in scattered farmhouses and barns and for the short time that they were there it did not rain. For the first time since leaving Thetford, five days before the horses were properly fed, watered and groomed.

The farriers were hard at work replacing shoes; Polly was one of many who had had shoes sucked off by the glutinous mud. The wheelwrights and carpenters and blacksmiths repaired the wagons and saddles and harnesses were cleaned and repaired. Bonfires made from any kind of dry fuel that could be found were lit, and blankets, rugs and the men's clothes were hung on hastily-erected lines to be dried.

That night, as Cupid stood, well-fed, clean and dry in the horse lines, she had her first experience of what was to become a far too familiar event.

The night was dry and the weather still; it felt as if there might be a frost, and the clouds were clearing and the odd star was appearing. Suddenly, flashes appeared on the horizon; was it lightning? Then she heard a distant rumble; surely not thunder on a cold, still night like this?

The ground vibrated and she was suddenly frightened. All the horses became restless as the ground trembled beneath them. The flashes became brighter and the reports louder. Cupid's mind flashed back to the practice ranges in England, and she realised that this was gunfire.

The men came out to watch as the sky lit up in front of them, and spoke quietly amongst each other; some came over to the horse lines to calm the horses and others just stood in silence as the realisation hit them that the front line was less than two miles away and they were witnessing an artillery barrage. They had no idea whose guns were firing, but for the next two hours it felt like the world was ending. Sadly, no doubt for some it had.

Suddenly the firing stopped, and then strange streaks appeared in the sky which burst into an eerie glow before drifting towards the ground. These were the Very lights that heralded an attack and before long the pop-pop of machine gun and rifle fire could be heard.

By dawn it was quiet again, and as if nothing had happened, the men appeared for morning stables and the horses were fed, watered and groomed.

Before long they were harnessed up and hooked in to the guns and wagons, or saddled up ready to move; another march had begun, this time through the forest of Nieppe.

Vernon sat silently on Cupid as they trudged on. He was deep in thought and had his pipe clenched between his teeth. How long before it would be their turn?

They stopped the night at Morbeque before moving on to a small town called Thiennes, where again the men were billeted in old farm buildings a short distance from the town near a village called Tannay, but the horse lines were in waterlogged fields, and it was raining again. The ground soon became a quaking mass of mud which the wretched horses had to stand in up to their hocks.

Although it was freezing cold the men would cast off their putties, boots and socks and leave them somewhere in the dry when they came to the horses, either to feed them, take them to water or, because orders were orders, to groom them (many a curry comb and dandy brush would be lost forever in the oozing mud). They would be barefoot because it was more bearable to clean and dry your freezing feet after your work was done and have dry socks, and half-dry boots to put on again than it was to live in permanently waterlogged boots.

Dotted about these disgusting fields were small dry islands which were stacked high with forage and bundles of harness covered with tarpaulins. To call them dry would be an overstatement, for the rain continued and the wind howled, tearing at the tarpaulins and forcing the rain under them.

Other creatures also took advantage of these 'havens'; huge rats scuttled back and forth stealing food and chewing holes in the sacks, which then burst when the men tried to carry them to feed the horses. Anything that was dropped into the mud was lost. There was nothing to boost the ever-sinking morale of the men, and nothing to be done to improve the health and wellbeing of the horses, which were suffering dreadfully.

The horses remained at Tannay in these wretched conditions until the 12th of December. The men, including Vernon, came and went; they took it in turns to be attached to regular Batteries in the line – this was their baptism of fire, and when they returned the looks on their stern, grey, frightened faces told their own story.

When the orders finally came to move, the task of pulling the guns and wagons out of the gun park was enormous. They had sunk into the glue-like mud, and it took extreme effort from both horses and men until at last they were ready to leave this godforsaken place.

The road took them past the scene of some recent fighting; there were shell holes everywhere and lying amongst them were the unburied and swollen corpses of horses and men. The burial parties had been unable to reach them in these appalling conditions.

Cupid had never seen or smelt anything like this before; it was truly shocking. She was a horse, she served man to the best of her ability, she liked and trusted most men and enjoyed being ridden by them. Vernon was her friend, or so she thought, but now she was confused; how could men do this to other men? Would she ever see a proper stable again, feel the sun on her back again, eat fresh green grass again, and gallop freely across country with a happy man on her back?

On they went. Their destination was a village called Ames just south west of Lillers, a day's journey away. None of the men spoke a word. An occasional order was barked out by an officer or NCO, usually because somebody was falling behind or some equipment had fallen off a wagon that had been badly loaded in the confusion earlier on. Cupid's back was sore, and Vernon sat on her like a dead weight; he was making no effort but kicked her occasionally, grumbling and coughing continuously. Most of the men were coughing; the cold and the wet had taken its toll.

The road took them past miles of ruined countryside and wrecked farms and through deserted villages where the houses were just heaps of rubble, churches were empty shells and the graveyards were pockmarked with shell holes. It was dusk when they reached Ames and thank God, dry! Ames was still intact, or virtually so; people still lived there and there was a faint air of normality.

Late that night when the horses had been fed, watered, cleaned and groomed properly for the first time for days, the men discovered the *estaminets* and cafés where they could buy coffee and rum.

That night as Cupid stood in the horse lines, warm and well fed, she could hear voices, the sort of voices that she hadn't heard for days, happy voices, laughter and eventually singing. As the men made their way back to their billets a group of them wandered down to the horse lines, puffing on Woodbines and Gold Flake or re-lighting their pipes, slightly tipsy.

It was the first time since they had left Thetford in November that both horses and men had been comfortable, and the men had come to have one last look at the horses before sleep.

Vernon, who was amongst them, walked quietly over to Cupid and slid his cold hands under her rug. Cupid was lucky to have a rug, as most of the horses had nothing. Vernon had found it abandoned in an old farm building and commandeered it immediately. He whispered into her ears, and she could smell the alcohol on his breath and hear the wheezing from his lungs. He was full of cold and desperately tired, but before he could sleep he had to make friends again with Cupid. After this he went to his billet and slept decently for the first time since arriving in France.

The Brigade remained at Ames until the 27th December. The horses were exercised every day, repairs were made as usual to the equipment and both horses and men began to recover from their ills.

On Christmas Day a church parade was held in the village square. The Padre preached a sermon and the men sang carols which drifted over the horse lines. Cupid's ears pricked up and she felt content.

Leaving early on the morning of the 27th December, the Brigade marched all day, arriving in the evening at Noeux les Mines; they were about to go into action and it was here that the guns were prepared and everything made ready. From here they marched on to the little ruined town of Vermelles. There was an air of anxiety and expectation and the men were edgy and alert. They were to relieve the Batteries of another Brigade and watched them as they withdrew from their position.

This part of the front was the scene of heavy and continuous fighting, and the enemy was so close that in some places the Germans held one end of a section of trench while the British held the other.

On the morning of the 28th December 1915 the Brigade went into action. The firing started and continued all day and all night, and huge quantities of ammunition were used. The Germans fired back; it was an artillery duel. The air was thick with smoke and Cupid's ears rang. Shrapnel flew through the air, the guns roared and the ammunition wagons rushed back and forth feeding the guns, it was a truly hellish scene.

Extraordinarily, on the evening of the 29th, orders came to

cease fire immediately and withdraw from action. The Brigade had expected a lengthy stay in this hell-hole, and though relieved at being withdrawn so soon, they were also surprised and confused.

The horses, wagons and limbers were ordered up from the wagon lines and in double time the Brigade pulled out of their positions, passing on the road the Brigade that they had relieved, which was now heading back into action. By nine o'clock the next morning they were back in Ames.

On New Year's Day 1916 they moved again, this time to the little town of Therouanne, a pleasant place to be and largely untouched by the war. The townsfolk were friendly and there were children running about the streets; they came to the horse lines to watch the men at work, feeding and grooming the horses. Occasionally the men would put the children up onto the horses and lead them up and down the street.

Vernon lifted a little girl up onto Cupid and as he ran leading Cupid, the girl laughed and called out to her mother to come and watch. Her mother called back and clapped, and although Cupid didn't recognise their language, she was happy too. The little featherweight on her back crying out with delight reminded her of the distant past, and of home, when the village children would be put on her back and taken down to the fields to watch the haymaking, taking with them a picnic and stone bottles of ginger beer, or homemade lemonade; she was happy and Vernon was happy. It was the first time she had heard him laugh for weeks.

Early in the morning of 11th January 1916, the Brigade were

preparing to move again. Everything was made ready and it wasn't long before the column was winding its way out of the town, eventually arriving at Berguette railway station, where they waited for many hours.

During this long wait, Cupid had a pleasant surprise; for the first time since leaving Le Havre, Nimrod reappeared. He had spent all this time with the ammunition column, on loan to another man. It was a pleasure to see him. He looked well, though a little thin.

Eventually, yet again, they were loaded on to a train; this time the train was not long enough to take all the horses and equipment, so the Brigade was split roughly in half. Luckily for Cupid she was led on to the same wagon as Flashlight, Polly and Nimrod, so at least she was amongst friends as she stood on the bare wooden floor of the rickety wagon.

Cupid had spent a few days short of two months in Northern France and seen sights that she never wished to see again. She had survived the appalling conditions, and now that she was being loaded on to a train again and had been reunited with Nimrod, she felt homesick and longed to return to the life she had been forced to abandon some eighteen months before. Perhaps this was the journey that would take her home.

A whistle blew, and the train began to move; slowly they chugged out of the station. It was raining again.

CHAPTER FOUR

❧

The train rattled on for three days and two nights. The trucks were closed, which made it impossible to see the country they were passing through, though Cupid felt that it was becoming warmer and the air dryer.

The train stopped briefly four times during the journey, at Dijon, Montreaux, Lyons and Avignon, where the horses were watered and the train re-coaled and watered; their measly nosebag rations were eaten on the move. Finally, during the afternoon of 14th January, they arrived at Marseilles.

Cupid emerged from the train into bright sunshine; she felt its warmth immediately. She looked about to see seagulls everywhere, just as at Southampton, but the weather was fine, the breeze warm and the sky blue. Where was she?

Cupid, Flashlight, Polly, Nimrod and all the other horses that had travelled with them were tied to a row of water troughs full of delicious fresh water. They watched while the men continued to unload the train; their own kitbags, then the guns and the general service wagons that had travelled with them. The rest would follow with the other horses over the next few days. Several hours later they were ready to go and with Vernon on her back, they left the station yard.

The long column of horses, guns and wagons wound its way slowly through the streets of Marseilles and then began to work its way uphill, leaving the town behind them. The sun shone, and its warmth was delicious compared to the cold, wet and miserable climate of northern France. The roads were dry and hard; there was no clinging mud or cavernous pot-holes.

After a short journey of about three or four miles they marched into La Valentin Camp. The camp was vast, but it was clean, tidy, efficiently-run and a comfortable place for both the horses and men. It was also beautifully situated up in the hills with distant views of the snow-capped Alps to the north east, and below them the city of Marseilles and the sparkling blue Mediterranean Sea.

Cupid had no idea where she was, but the sight of the green grass and the tall trees unspoilt by the ravages of war and the cloudless blue sky gave her a feeling of intense pleasure. She, Polly, Nimrod and Flashlight were happily installed in clean, dry horse lines with a seemingly endless supply of fresh water and a healthy amount of good feed unspoilt by rain, mud and rats.

La Valentin Camp was a bustling place, crammed full of men and horses that had travelled from all parts of the British Empire, many from Australia, New Zealand and India. Marseilles docks were a hub of activity. Ships came and went twenty four hours a day, bringing supplies of military hardware, men and horses from halfway around the world to supply the vicious, unending and relentless appetite of the Western Front.

On the 29th January the remainder of the horses and equipment that had been left behind in the north arrived by train at Marseilles, and were soon brought up to the camp. These horses were immediately segregated and subjected to yet another veterinary inspection, the results of which were disastrous. The horses had been tested for glanders, a particularly nasty, malignant, contagious and fatal disease of horses. The results were positive; the worst result possible.

Every one of the horses that had arrived that day had to be destroyed, causing great unhappiness amongst the men; many of these horses had been with them since the beginning of the war and were old friends who knew their work. It was the men who had looked after them, trained with them and nursed them through the recent horrors of the front line who had to carry out this unpleasant task. Although the weather was fine and the sky was blue, it seemed that a black cloud was hanging over La Valentin Camp on the last three days of January 1916.

Mercifully, the horses that had arrived earlier in the month, including Cupid, Flashlight, Polly and Nimrod, were found to be free of the disease and allowed to live; otherwise Cupid's story would have ended here in the hills above Marseilles with so many of her companions.

As a result of this disaster, much of the Brigade had to be re-horsed, which caused a considerable delay to any future movements. The remounts arrived over the next few days; there was a 'Remount Depot' close by which provided remounts for the Australian and Indian Cavalry on their way north to the Front, and it was from here that the new horses were acquired.

When the first of these new horses arrived it caused quite a stir amongst the other residents of the horse lines. In the main they were big, well-built horses, but bad-mannered and they tended to unsettle the others; there was much kicking, biting and other boorish behaviour which frankly neither the old horses or the men were accustomed to, having been together for so long.

These new horses were known as 'Walers' and were horses bred in New South Wales, Australia and then imported into Britain via India. Since the beginning of the war they had been arriving in their thousands, such was the need for remounts as a result of the shocking wastage of the Western Front.

The delay did however result in a few more days of comfortable living for Cupid and her friends. The weather remained settled and the sun shone and despite the initial excitement caused by the new arrivals, La Valentin Camp was, in Cupid's mind, the best place that they had been since August 1914.

One morning during this extended period of good living, Vernon arrived at the horse lines to take Cupid out for exercise; with him was another newcomer, a small, sandy-coloured, mongrel terrier. Before they could be introduced, the terrier flew at Cupid's heels. Cupid, who had been brought up with dogs and hounds, took absolutely no notice of this childish behaviour, which caused much indignation to the dog, which had no doubt been hoping to cause as much chaos as possible; such is the mind of the terrier.

After several expletives from Vernon, which the dog, being French, obviously didn't understand, order was restored, and a formal introduction took place.

On the previous evening Vernon and several of his pals had gone into Marseilles for food and refreshment, and on their return, after a glass or two of the local brandy, they discovered that they were being followed by the dog; no encouragement would persuade the dog to go home and before long it was inside the camp, and asleep on Vernon's bed. The dog, although French, was immediately named 'Bosche' by Vernon and the following morning, after sharing his breakfast, it had followed him to the horse lines.

For an hour and a half they rode through the hills above Marseilles, the warm spring sunshine on their backs. Cupid was content; she seemed back in her natural environment, Vernon happily on her back and a little dog trotting along beside them, just as life had been before the war. The only reminder of war was when they stopped at the top of the hill and looked out over the sparkling sea; there were ships everywhere, and they could see the smoke from their funnels disappearing over the horizon.

There were troop ships, cargo ships and oil tankers plying their way to and from Marseilles, all escorted by warships; these were happy hunting grounds for German submarines.

Bosche and Vernon became inseparable; everywhere he went, the dog went too, and he became more amenable and obedient by the day.

On the 7th February 1916 La Valentin Camp became a hive of activity. Wagons were loaded, guns dragged from the gun park and made ready to be hooked into, and the men checked and double checked their kit; they were making ready to move again.

The next morning the Brigade departed La Valentin Camp, the long column winding its way back down the hill and into Marseilles, eventually forming up at the docks. It took the whole day to embark onto two ships, the SS *Andiana* and the SS *Maryland*.

The three and a half weeks that Cupid and her companions had spent at La Valentin Camp had done them a power of good.

The sunshine and the sea air, together with proper food rations and exercise, had been a great tonic.

The horses and the men were now in good shape. Even the 'Walers' had settled down and were now pulling their weight. In fact the men were very impressed with these wonderful horses that had travelled so far across the world. It was only Nimrod who still seemed a little weak; he hadn't put on weight and remained rather sluggish. However the vets had passed him fit for duty and he stood quietly with the others on the dockside.

The whole process of loading the ships was much calmer and more efficient than it had been on that awful morning at Southampton in November. Cupid, Flashlight, Polly and Nimrod were loaded together onto the Andiana, but as soon as they passed through the ominous black hole in the ship's side, the memories came flooding back; the unpleasant smells, the stale air and the strange echoing, booming noises once again caused them to feel nervous and uncomfortable.

Before long they heard the hatch being winched shut; there were frightful squeals as the rusty hinges began to move and then the loud crash as the huge door finally closed. Soon afterwards the judder of the propellers starting to turn, and then the awful swaying motion began.

CHAPTER FIVE

❧

The Brigade were at sea for four days. The Andiana had left Marseilles before the Maryland as the ships had had to wait for their escort destroyers to nurse them on their journey across the Mediterranean.

The conditions on the horse-decks were frightful; it got hotter and hotter and the air staler and more unhealthy by the hour. The strong stink of ammonia from the horse dung made life a misery; it caught in the throat and stung the eyes.

Although they were lucky that the sea was calm, the continuous rolling of the ship put the horses off their food, which again was a measly dry ration delivered in a nosebag. The water that came twice a day in a bucket carried by the sweating men was warm and unpalatable and several of the horses refused to drink, although their thirst must have been raging in these awful conditions.

The men worked hard to keep the horses as clean and comfortable as possible and to encourage them to drink; it was essential to keep them hydrated. They would appear in shifts and remain with the horses for as long as they could, cleaning out scupper drains to try and get rid of the horse urine that was making the air so foul, sometimes hosing down the deck with pumped sea water. When they could take no more of this poisonous atmosphere they would head back up onto the deck into the fresh air and the next shift would take its turn.

On the second morning several of the horses had collapsed, weakened from lack of water and food, especially water; the men worked tirelessly to try and get them back on their feet, but generally this was in vain and the only option was to shoot the poor creatures to end their suffering. The echoing crack from a .45 revolver was heard more than a few times that morning, the noise amplified in the confined quarters of the horse decks.

Later that morning Vernon came running past Cupid with a few other men; poor old Nimrod had collapsed. Cupid had sensed that he was not right when they had been loaded onto the ship. He was thin and unsteady on his legs; he hadn't eaten once during the journey and had drunk very little.

They battled for nearly an hour to get him up before the shot rang out. The horse deck went strangely quiet after the echo had died away. Then Vernon came up to Cupid and stroked her nose, tears streaming down his cheeks.

The smell of the fresh blood unsettled the horses and after Nimrod's corpse had been dragged away by the men, the deck was hosed down again with seawater and scrubbed clean. Cupid's happy memories of her time at La Valentin Camp were fast ebbing away.

Before long the corpse was winched up onto the deck through a hatch and then dragged and manhandled over the side and into the sea. Nimrod was the third horse to go over the side that day. Vernon, his shirt drenched with sweat from the hard work, leaned on the ships rails and watched him float away; his pipe was clenched between his teeth and the tears still streamed down his cheeks.

Later that day the horse decks were filled with loud and continuous booming noises which didn't help to settle the horses, or the men who were with them. The gunners were firing their 18-pounder guns from the deck at wooden barrels that had been thrown over the side, the first time they had fired a gun since they had been withdrawn from the Front in January.

Both Vernon and his father wrote letters home from the ship. Vernon wrote earlier on the voyage, clearly before Nimrod's sad demise:

So far we have had an excellent voyage the sea has been a bit bumpy on one or two occasions, and made some of the men sick but I am glad to say that I have not yet been affected. It is pretty hot for the horses down in the holds of the ship, but I hope we shall manage to get to our destination without losing any. I have managed to get hold of a dog now, and have him on board with me, he is about the size of a large fox terrier, and is the colour and hair rather like a chow, a topping little beast, the only crab is a curly tail rather like a pig. He is much better behaved than Vanity [the dog that he had left at home] *he follows me well and lies down under my seat quite quietly.*

His father writes slightly later in the journey:

We have all four of our 18pr guns in action on the decks, and the ship has another at the stern. We practised with our guns one day at a barrel thrown overboard and did good shooting – but marine shooting with a rolling ship going 15 miles an hour isn't so awfully easy. Horses have suffered from heat down below – we have lost 3, but that is a low average. The boy has a strong stomach & spends his entire time down in the lower stable decks cleaning out skupper drain holes, and comes into my cabin, which I share with him, stinking of the most putrid smells that I have yet run across – only the strongest stomachs can face those lower regions for long, he picked up a mongrel yellow terrier dog at our last place & has it here - it also stinks and lives in my cabin, it has a curly tail and is called Bosche.

At last, late in the afternoon of 12th February, the *Andiana* berthed at Alexandria, and not an hour too soon; three more horses had been lost during the last day of the journey and the men and horses were in a sorry state. Fresh water was running low and the foul atmosphere in the horse decks was now almost unbearable. Despite this, the disembarkation did not begin until 9.30 on the evening of the 14th.

Finally the unsteady horses were led down the gangway and onto the dockside; it was dark and not easy to see their new surroundings, but the strange new smells of Egypt were mystifying and, after the putrid air that they had been breathing aboard the ship, wonderful. Shortly afterwards, Vernon appeared, Bosche trotting along at his heels.

They were not long enough at Alexandria to see the spacious harbour for by midnight, after being watered, the horses were again being loaded onto a train; thankfully the trucks were open and the horses relished the dry, chilly air. Mercifully this was to be a short rail journey and at three o'clock in the morning the train pulled into the station at Cairo.

It was daylight by the time the train was unloaded and the

horses fed and watered, after which the Brigade was formed into a column and they marched out of the station yard.

As they entered the streets of Cairo, Cupid was overwhelmed by her new surroundings; there were strange square, flat-topped white buildings, which seemed to shine in the bright early sunlight. There were people everywhere in all sorts of strange clothes, some in bright colours and others in pure white; in fact the whole place seemed ablaze with colour.

There were loud cries from people sitting at the roadside selling oranges and a multitude of other commodities, their target audience being the khaki-clad British and Australian soldiers that were intermingling with the locals.

There were people leading donkeys which had vast piles of all sorts tied onto their backs, anything from firewood to furniture; some were being ridden, the Egyptian men sitting well back on the animal's haunches with their feet trailing along the ground, while their wives walked beside them. This old-fashioned scene was suddenly disturbed when a bell rang to clear the street and a modern electric tram rushed by.

As the street widened, one of the horses that was being led by a soldier riding in front of Cupid and Vernon stretched its neck out to try and take a bite from what looked like a large pile of green forage dumped in the middle of the road. At that moment the pile of green heaved itself up into the air. It was attached to the back of a camel which had been squatting underneath it, and was hidden by its huge load; Cupid had never seen such a terrifying sight in all her life, and leapt into the air, nearly throwing Vernon to the ground. What was this hideous animal?

The camel, much put out by being disturbed, turned its head and spat at Cupid and her rider.

As they continued their journey, more and more of these strange creatures appeared on the street, some carrying enormous loads on their strangely-shaped backs and moving along with a curious lurching gait. The horses found them very unsettling and Cupid in particular was positively scared of them. Little did they realise what a lifeline these amazing creatures would be to them in the coming months.

In front of them was a huge river, beside which were large areas of green fertile ground. The land was being worked by boys who walked behind wooden ploughs that were dragged by very docile-looking water buffaloes. This was another sight that amazed Cupid; she was accustomed to cows and had known them all her life, but these strange creatures ploughing the land were a mystery to her.

The long column crossed the Nile by the Kasr-el-Nil Bridge and then swung south onto a long straight road that took them to their new camp about nine miles south east of Cairo; the new camp was called Mena Camp. Cupid looked about at her new surroundings; on one side were the green cultivated lands of the Nile Delta and on the other the emptiness of the sandy desert, out of which loomed the vast shapes of the Pyramids. The sun shone, casting strange shadows across the sand hills that made up this peculiar landscape, which was to be their home for the next six weeks or so.

When the Brigade arrived at Mena Camp, the area they were to occupy was actually nothing more than a campsite in the desert; the men had to 'pitch' their camp.

The horses were corralled into enclosures made from stakes and rope, while the men erected the more permanent horse lines in which they were to live. Tents were put up in rows and it wasn't long before Mena Camp took on the appearance of a canvas city.

On 11th February 1916, Vernon's father, who was now commanding the Brigade, wrote to his wife:

I am writing this in my Bde. Office tent, pitched on the desert sand about 9 miles SE of Cairo, almost under the shadows of the Pyramids – a view too glorious to describe, one way the green cultivation of the Nile Delta & the other the sand hills of the desert. The sun is brilliant, and hot during the day, the sunset is perfectly glorious, and the nights very cold. We had a very tiring journey here. We entrained at Alexandria at once, & after 5 ½ hours we arrived at Cairo at 3.30 A.M. having to hook in at once & drive our tired unfit horses 9 miles to camp – or rather to ground where we had to pitch our camp. Since then we have had a scramble to get ourselves settled & prepared for the rest of the Divisional Artillery who are arriving at all hours. Our horses are pretty well considering the awful travelling we have had and Flashlight & Cupid & Polly are all fit.

The first weeks spent at Mena camp were varied, and it took time for the horses to get used to their new surroundings; they were ridden every day round the Pyramids, which were about a mile away from the camp, and sometimes further afield to where there were ancient tombs and ruins which much interested the men but were dull for the horses, as they were often left standing in the sun while the men went to inspect these strange-looking remains. Also the flies were starting to become a nuisance, although they were nothing to what they would become later on.

Besides this, wherever they went there were camels, and for some reason these animals unsettled the horses more than anything else.

Life in the camp was actually very comfortable for the horses. Food was plentiful and there was a permanent supply of fresh water pumped from the Nile into long wooden watering troughs that the men had built close to the horse lines. The sun shone and the temperature rose daily.

On 14th February Vernon's father wrote again:

In the evenings we ride round the Pyramids, and the Sphinx, and our horses are very scared with the camels, yesterday some of us rode about 9 miles across the desert & saw some wonderful temples and tombs, about 5000 years old, and all the lovely carvings and painting as good as when they were done.

Having left England, suffered the deprivations of the Western Front, enjoyed the relief of those few weeks at Marseille and now arrived in the hot sandy Egyptian desert, the horses needed to be clipped. Their winter coats had grown long and shaggy and were beginning to die back. The men began the arduous task of clipping; it was a painfully slow job as there were so many hundreds of horses, and hand clipping was the only option.

Eventually local Arabs were employed to help; these people were naturally good with the horses. They were calm and efficient, spoke quietly in a strange language, which seemed to settle the horses and made the job so much easier. Also they had their own clipping machines, worked by two men, one to wind the handle which drove the clipping machine while the other clipped the horse. These local Arabs could clip about eight horses a day by hand, and about twenty-five by machine, for a shilling each.

At last Cupid's turn came; she had been clipped many times before and so stood calmly while the men did their work, and the relief of getting rid of her long shaggy, dying winter coat was wonderful. Yet although the days became hotter and hotter, the Egyptian nights were chilly. Sometimes the temperature would drop close to freezing, and the horses would huddle together under the clear, starry skies.

Cupid and Vernon, Polly, and Flashlight soon got used to this new lifestyle and Vernon would ride Cupid for miles over the desert sands. They were both becoming fitter by the day and more acclimatised to this strange new land.

Each day all the horses would be exercised, and they were soon fitter than they had been since before leaving England; but it wasn't always an easy life. On some days the guns would be dragged out into the desert to practise firing. This was a noisy, tiring operation and great effort was needed from the horses and men to pull the guns and ammunition wagons through the desert sand. Their narrow wheels would sink into the soft sand, and the digging and pulling was exhausting in the intense heat of the Egyptian sun. Sometimes a sandstorm would blow up from nowhere; the sand would get everywhere, stinging the horses' eyes and filling their nostrils. The men would try to gently wipe it away, but it was impossible until the storm blew over.

Sunburn was another painful problem; the men wore thin uniforms, some of them short trousers, and their sleeves would be rolled up. These young men who had arrived here from an English winter and the chilling, oozing mud of Northern France would burn to a frazzle. Their skin would peel off in sheets and many became seriously ill; there was no protecting sun lotion in 1916.

Some of the horses' noses would also burn and the men would rub a sort of lanolin lotion onto the burns, most probably the same lotion they used on their own burnt skin, to try and ease the soreness. That was probably a mistake as their noses seemed to heal quickly, and afterwards would not burn again; the lanolin probably didn't help much, but the men would try anything to keep their horses comfortable.

The flies became worse and the horses were made to wear fly fringes on their brow-bands; these hung almost over the eyes and Cupid hated wearing them. She thought them almost as big a nuisance as the flies, but at least they prevented the eyes becoming infected. Many of the horses developed running sores in their eyes from the swarms of flies; this was an itchy, insect-ridden country and neither the men or the horses were used to such things.

During the first week of March 1916, an unusual thing happened which caused much excitement on the horse lines, especially amongst the mares; one of the mares foaled during the night. Cupid and Polly couldn't wait to meet the little newcomer. Nobody had been aware that one of the other mares was even in foal or indeed knew how she got in foal, having been on active service for so long. Nobody knew who the father was, but the two girls were quite put out by Flashlight's indifference to the new arrival.

On some days the men would race their horses around a track they had formed in the desert; sometimes it would be a flat race, and on other times it would be over jumps made from hurdles, or any other surplus equipment that could be found. The competition was fierce. On 2nd April 1916 both Cupid and Polly won their races, much to the delight of Vernon and his father, who rode Polly.

Vernon's father records this in a letter written on 3rd April 1916:

Vernon & I each rode a race yesterday & each of us won! In our Brigade there has been a great access of horseyness & they've all been racing against each other. I rode my brown mare yesterday and took on the champion & beat him but he was carrying more weight than I was. Vernon rode his pony against the champion of the smaller class of animal & won fairly easily - & the weights were about level.

Vernon's father still referred to Cupid as a pony, ever since he had given her to him as a fifteenth birthday present all that time ago.

The very next day, Monday 3rd April, the men began to strike camp; everything was packed up, tents, wagons, guns, ammunition, nothing was left behind. As the Brigade prepared to move off, one last thing was to happen before they departed from this famous part of Egypt. A large motorcar appeared down the bumpy road from Cairo carrying two men; the car drove about for a while with one of the men standing in the back.

The car had no roof, but had a sort of gantry built up over it to form a platform. The man in the back was a photographer from Cairo; his assistant drove him about while he looked to find the perfect position from which to take photographs of the Brigade with the Pyramids as the background.

Eventually, when he found the required position, the car stopped and the two men started to set up their equipment on top of the gantry. Each of the three Batteries in the Brigade would take its turn to be photographed, a lengthy operation under the piercing heat of the sun. They waited for what seemed an eternity while the man tweaked this and adjusted that, the sweat streamed off the men and the horses became bored standing in the heat. Eventually Cupid's turn came and after several attempts, a fine photograph was taken.

At long last the man finished, and shortly afterwards the Brigade formed up into a long column and headed north under a vast cloud of dust, back to Cairo, where on the evening of 4th April they again boarded a train. Thankfully for Cupid and her friends, the open-topped wagons had canvas roofs to shelter them from the piercing heat of the sun before it at last sank down over the western horizon like a huge red fireball.

After they had arrived at the railway station, and while the train was being loaded, Vernon and Cupid had one last job to do.

During the time that they had spent at Mena, no dogs had been allowed in the camp, for fear of rabies, so Bosche had spent the time at an SPCA home in Cairo. Cupid and Vernon went to collect Bosche, and were amazed at the variety of animals they saw being looked after by the society; there were a few hundred horses, dozens of mules and donkeys, a camel or two, plenty of dogs, and to Cupid's amazement, a creature that she had never seen before, a kangaroo belonging to an Australian regiment!

Bosche and Vernon were very pleased to be reunited, and the little dog trotted along at Cupid's heels all the way back to the railway station.

CHAPTER SIX

✣

The journey was long, hot and dusty and after many hours the train finally rattled into a station. They had arrived at the railhead at El Kubri, a post on the Suez Canal a short distance from Suez itself. The place bustled with activity, with hundreds of troops and thousands of horses being transferred to different parts of this strange new world.

After the arduous task of unloading, the horses were at last fed and watered and then immediately harnessed up; Vernon appeared with his saddle, saddlebags, and all his other light belongings with Bosche at his heel. He was soon up on Cupid's back and they began the slow march north to El Shatt, situated next to the canal and on the edge of the Sinai desert.

At first the track was firm and the going fairly easy, but after a while it petered out and became nothing more than soft sandy desert. The shade temperature was well over 100 degrees, and as the guns and wagons sank into the sand, the effort required from both horses and men was enormous.

The supply of water was a huge problem. There were some local wells which provided plenty, but it was brackish and although the horses were craving with thirst, it was hard to make them to drink enough, and they quickly lost condition.

It was here for the first time that they realised how important camels would be to their survival in the desert. Dozens of camels with Arab drivers were employed to bring fresh water up from wells that were close to the canal. The camels carried all the water for both the men and the horses. Each camel would carry two copper tanks known as 'fantasses' on its back; each tank contained nine gallons of water.

Hundreds of camels were used for this work and they plied endlessly back and forth. The water would come out of these tanks as hot as bath water and it would then be syphoned into large earthenware jars where it would cool by process of evaporation; this system was however only used for the men's drinking water while at camp.

Camels would also carry the forage for the horses, and luckily there was plenty of it; this was also brought up from the canal zone. It consisted of a type of green corn, unthrashed oat straw and hay which reminded Cupid of the clover hay she used to eat at home in those happy days before the war.

The horses were now much more used to the camels; they would sometimes stand near each other on the horse lines at night, or rather the camels would lie while the horses stood.

Whilst at the horse lines, either waiting to be watered or fed, Cupid would notice many of the strange creatures which lived in the desert. There were one or two strange crow-like birds that would scavenge on the refuse heaps; there were some large ants that would roll bits of horse dung away to their nests, and strange-looking lizards that would scuttle back and forth across the sand. It was indeed a strange new world for a horse brought up in the green pastures of Essex.

From this first week in April, the Brigade remained as part of the defence of the Suez Canal against a possible Turkish attack from Palestine. The Suez Canal was a vital supply route for Britain and her allies; supplies and reinforcements would pass through the canal from India, Australia, New Zealand and many other parts of the British Empire.

The Turks were keen to disrupt these supplies, and assist their German allies on the Western Front, and the Germans were keen to keep the British busy on this front to prevent them from sending reinforcements to France.

The routes across the Sinai desert from Palestine, which the Turks could use to launch an attack, were the old caravan tracks that had been used for centuries by nomads and pilgrims. It was on these tracks that the guns would be positioned to ambush any Turkish forces.

These gun positions had to be dug into the sand, and to accomplish this the day's work would start at three or four o'clock in the morning, in order to achieve as much as possible before the piercing heat of the midday sun caused all work to stop.

This was also the season when the *khamsin* winds would blow from the desert; these fierce winds were hot and dry and they would bring with them endless sandstorms. Great walls of sand some 20ft high would appear from nowhere and literally cover everything. The sand would sting the face, get into the eyes, get under the clothes, nothing was spared. The horses hated these storms. Fortunately they would end as quickly as they came, but clearing up the mess they caused made double the work and on many days the shade temperature would be 110 degrees or more.

The horses seemed to cope better than the men in these

furnace-like conditions, provided of course that there was always enough water, and it was the camels that provided this lifeline. Without them survival in the desert would have been impossible. Many of the men became sick from the heat, the flies were infernal and it was very hard to keep the food in an edible condition. Dysentery was becoming all too common and any cuts or sores caused by the hard physical work would quickly become infected. Sandfly fever was rife amongst the men and the military hospital at Suez was overrun.

All the camp refuse was burnt and great fires would smoulder day in and day out. The pressures put upon the men and horses were as tough as any battlefield, apart from the fact that nobody, at this stage at least, was shooting at them.

Cupid and Vernon, and men from all the Batteries, would ride for miles across the shimmering desert sand, sometimes covering twenty miles or more in a day, reconnoitring defensive positions for the guns. When found and deemed suitable by the higher powers, they would be dug out and the guns hauled into position. Everything had to be dug in and camouflaged, the guns, the ammunition wagons, the supply wagons carrying food for the men and essentially the water supply. Once it was completed the horses would return to the camp, where they would remain until the guns were moved again. Sometimes this would be days, sometimes weeks.

Each Battery would occasionally be given a few days' rest, and they would go back down to the banks of the canal, where the air was cooler. Cupid loved these short breaks. The horses were let loose into fenced areas, like large sandy fields with water troughs dotted about which were kept full by locals employed by the army.

The rest was blissful; Cupid would roll in the sand and then shake it out of her coat. It felt like a sort of massage.

The men would also have time to play, and they would hold competitions between their horses. They would race them or test them over jumps, making the obstacles higher and higher. The winning horse would be feted – until the next time.

The men adored their horses; they had been together for so long and shared so much over the last two years, and these happy times were a relief to both man and beast.

Someone else who enjoyed these breaks beside the canal was Bosche. He would follow Vernon and his companions down to the canal bank, where they would swim. Bosche loved the water as much as the men did. He had become a sort of mascot in the Battery and was well looked after by them all.

During these rest periods beside the canal, the men would watch the ships passing by. There were huge warships, ocean liners converted into troop carriers, cargo vessels and even the occasional submarine. The ships were so close to the bank that their names could be read and whenever a ship registered in Tilbury passed by, a great cheer would go up. Tilbury was the local town for many of these South Essex men, and just the sight of that name would make them think of home.

The Brigade remained dotted about between various desert outposts for several weeks, and the work done by the horses became more and more monotonous. The days spent wearily trudging across the desert seemed to merge into one. The endless sandstorms and the relentless swarms of flies made life close to unbearable; even at night the air was always foul from the stink of the burning camp refuse. Cupid longed for those precious few days of rest, which came all too seldom, but here they were and here they had to stay, at least for the time being.

There were rumours going about that the enemy were preparing for some sort of attack, and there had indeed been one or two small skirmishes to the north of them, the news of which caused much chatter amongst the men and made everybody more alert. The rumours intensified between May and August and eventually the expeditions into the desert ceased and the whole Brigade was again concentrated in the camp at El Shatt.

It was vital that the Suez Canal remained open; any disruption to this essential supply route would have a catastrophic effect on the Allied forces in Europe. Gun pits were dug into the banks of the canal and the Brigade was put on high alert, every effort being made to gather information about a possible attack.

One of the greatest risks was sabotage; a night raid to mine the canal would have been very difficult to detect and if it succeeded, a sunken ship could block the narrow stretch of water for days, probably weeks.

Therefore a cunning plan was put into action. Each evening before the sun set, teams of horses were sent out with their drivers to the edge of the desert where, using a heavy sweep, they would harrow an area of ground between the desert and the canal, an area too wide for anything to cross without leaving a track mark in the sand. At dawn this great harrowed path would be inspected and no ships would be allowed to pass through the canal until the inspection teams were certain that nobody and nothing had passed over it during the night, and the all clear was given.

The horses that were used for this operation were usually employed pulling guns or wagons, but the work was easy for them. Many of them been farm horses before the war and pulling a set of harrows through the soft sand was second nature, even if the harrows and whippletrees were homemade and muddled together from bits and pieces of surplus military equipment.

Cupid and her friends would watch the teams leaving the camp under a cloud of dust as they stood at the watering troughs after their evening feed. It was a peaceful scene, and they would listen to the men coaxing the horses on as they disappeared out of sight.

Apart from the state of high alert, life in the camp was more comfortable than it had been of late; fresh water was plentiful and the forage rations for the horses excellent. Although the heat at midday was sometimes hardly bearable, at least the sandstorms were less frequent, which was a great relief to the horses, although the flies remained a constant irritation.

The men's tents were pitched on the banks of the canal which was pleasant for them too as there was good swimming, much enjoyed by Bosche and Vernon.

Thus life continued with almost boring regularity until early in the morning of 20th July 1916. The men were just finishing their morning stables. Some of the horses had been fed and were now at the watering troughs, some were still feeding and others were being groomed. The blacksmiths were doing their rounds, one or two of the horses whose coats had become shaggy again were being clipped and the men who had finished first were lining up outside the cookhouse for their breakfast.

Cupid, Polly and Flashlight had been fed and were beside each other at the water troughs when a distant droning noise was heard. The horses at first took not much notice of this unfamiliar sound, until suddenly there was a shout from a man who was looking up into the sky. "Aeroplanes!" he shouted, pointing up into the air.

There were two aircraft, both of them German Taubes, strange-looking machines in the shape of a dove. They were monoplanes and carried two people, the pilot and the bomber. The Taube was already considered to be rather out of date in 1916, but it still had the capacity to be lethal.

The two aircraft circled high above the camp for a short time and nobody really seemed to know what to do. There was a good deal of shouting and more pointing. Since their arrival in Egypt they had seen very few aircraft, and the ones that had occasionally appeared had been British.

The planes circled one more time and then flew east over the desert into the rising sun. The men, squinting their eyes against the sun, continued to watch them until suddenly they turned, came lower and headed back towards the camp. As they came closer, an officer wearing a pair of coloured goggles to protect his eyes from the sun peered through a pair of binoculars and spotted the dark black crosses on the underside of the wings.

"They're Huns!" he shouted, and at the same time started to fumble for his revolver, which he then fired at the approaching aircraft in a hopeless attempt to turn them away. The sudden commotion unsettled the horses and several that were being led to water bolted. Cupid and her friends took fright and struggled to free themselves from the rail to which they were tied. The troughs collapsed and the water cascaded out onto the desert sand.

By this time the aircraft were above them. They dropped their bombs, the massive explosions obliterating all other sound as the bombs hit their target.

The aeroplanes had vanished by the time the dust had settled and the grim results of this surprise attack became apparent.

Mercifully only one man was killed, but eight were badly wounded. It was by great good fortune that Cupid and her friends had been at the watering lines at the time of the attack. They were completely unscathed, though very rattled, and stood shakily amongst the remains of the troughs.

Not far away, the damage to the horse lines and camel lines was severe. Ten horses had been killed and thirty-two camels, while many others suffered nasty shrapnel wounds.

The next few days were spent gloomily tidying up and repairing the damage. The dead horses and camels were buried in the sand and the wounded horses were tended to. The war had caught up with them again for the first time since they had been withdrawn from the front line in France seven months before.

Cupid and her companions were to remain in these parts until the end of the year. Daily life became monotonous; although there was a constant state of alert, any skirmishing that happened was further to the north. A few more attempts were made by the enemy to drop bombs onto, or near, the canal, but the bombs fell harmlessly into the desert. One of the 18-pounder guns was built up onto a platform and fired at the approaching aeroplanes. It never did hit anything, but it certainly deterred the enemy fliers from coming too close.

During the autumn the weather became slightly cooler, the

temperature hovering in the nineties, but the air became stickier and more oppressive. The men consequently became bad tempered; they were homesick and felt that they had been forgotten while the war raged on in France.

The horses also became less fit, some of them even growing quite fat. They too suffered from the muggy conditions, and any work they were asked to do seemed twice as hard. Often the skies were grey and there was no breeze, which made the flies even more unbearable, and the stench of the burning camp refuse hung heavily in the air, adding to the gloom.

CHAPTER SEVEN

❧

It was not until the first week of January 1917 that anything much happened to change or improve their lives. Nine months had passed since they had arrived in this strange world on the banks of the Suez Canal.

During this first week the men started to dismantle the camp, the wagons were loaded, piled high with equipment; Cupid watched as the men worked away and she noticed a small group of men building a makeshift cage on the back of one of the wagons. They lined the bottom with straw and then put in a bowl of water. When they had finished, a man appeared carrying a large and contented-looking goose.

The men had caught the goose the day before on the banks of the Canal, they had tempted it into a box with a few crusts of bread and had kept it overnight in one of their tents. Goose eggs could be a tasty supplement to army rations. The goose was christened Lordy. It was yet to be found out whether it was in fact a goose or a gander, but either way it would soon become a friend to the men, the horses and to Bosche.

By the end of the week the Brigade was ready to move. Their time here was over and the next stage of Cupid's journey was about to begin.

At 5.30 in the morning on 9th January 1917 they marched away from El Shatt. It was a slow march; none of the horses were very fit, having been in the same place for so long, as it had been difficult to give them enough exercise in the confines of the camp.

On they went, arriving at 9.15 the following morning at the railway station at El Kubri, which was just the same as it had been in April the previous year, except that there seemed to be even more men, horses and equipment being marshalled this way and that.

The horses were exhausted when they arrived; they had only been watered once in the last twenty-four hours and had had only one measly feed from a nosebag. The water and transport camels had been left behind at El Shatt.

A long train rattled into the station and a few hours later, Cupid was again loaded onto a wagon and another railway journey had begun.

As the train headed north, it was painfully slow and the heat torturous. Cupid was craving water. Her legs trembled and she found it hard to stand as the wagon rocked and swayed over the uneven track.

Seven hours later they arrived at a place called Moascar on the edge of the desert, not far from Ismailia. Moascar was a vast camp, full of soldiers from all corners of the British Empire; there were Australians, Indians, even Gurkhas, as well as huge numbers of British troops.

It took an age to unload the train and it wasn't until they had got into the camp that at last the horses were watered; the last thirty-six hours had been very trying.

The Brigade remained at Moascar for about three weeks and it was here that it was re-equipped and brought up to fighting strength. They were making ready for the long march across the desert to Palestine.

The men worked hard. The wheels of the guns and wagons were fitted with 'pedrails', flat wooden blocks about ten inches square that were attached around the tyre of the wheel with chains. They were arranged so that as the wheel turned, the pedrails would be in a flat position when they reached the ground, giving the wheels a larger surface area and thus distributing the weight over more ground and preventing them from sinking so far into the soft sand.

Especially long draught-bars were made by the blacksmiths and fitted to the limbers; this was to allow four horses to be in draught abreast when pulling the guns and ammunition wagons, meaning that each one would now be pulled by a team of twelve horses instead of the usual six.

When the time came to leave the camp at Moascar, the Brigade consisted of some 650 men, over 700 horses, several dogs, including Bosche, and a goose. Bosche now travelled with the ammunition column and he much enjoyed the comfort, lying in the sun on top of one of the wagons and being spoilt rotten by the men who drove them. However this meant that he would have very little contact with Cupid and Vernon for the duration of this long journey.

The long column marched away from Moascar on 31st January 1917, heading north for Kantara and then El Gilban, which they reached on 2nd February. Here the men bivouacked for the night.

Leaving El Gilban at nine o'clock on the morning of 3rd

February, they headed west, following the old caravan track, which would eventually lead them into Palestine; at intervals along this track there were fresh-water wells which dictated the length of each day's march. No water was carried for the horses, so arrival at these wells was a wonderful relief for the wretched animals.

Cupid and her Brigade were now part of a huge army heading towards Palestine. To keep such a vast number of men and horses supplied with water and rations was a logistical nightmare. As the army moved east, engineers were laying a railway across the desert to bring up supplies of water, food and equipment. Sandstorms would daily cover the newly-laid track with great drifts of sand which had to be shovelled away before work could be resumed, but despite these difficulties the railway grew longer by the day. At the same times, a pipeline was being laid which would eventually pump water from the Nile all the way into Palestine, a remarkable feat of engineering undertaken in a very short space of time in the most arduous and exhausting conditions.

The engineers also built a 'wire road', a layer of wire mesh that had been laid onto the desert sand to provide a firm surface on which to travel. It was however for the sole use of the Infantry. The Artillery had to drag itself through the soft sand.

Another trouble for both the men and horses was that although the days were hot, this was February and the nights could become very cold. Strong north-westerly winds blew inland from the Mediterranean Sea to add to their discomfort. The men shivered as they tried to sleep under their bivouacs wrapped in the one blanket that they were allowed and the horses stood huddled together at the horse lines.

On 4th February they reached Romani after a journey of only

seven miles, which had taken a whole day to complete due to the rough country over which they were traveling; the men and the horses were exhausted.

The new railway had reached Romani but thus far it only carried enough fresh water for the men; once the men had found their camping ground, the horses had to be ridden or led to the wells beneath a sandy hill known as Katib Gannet nearly two miles away. The wells provided plenty of water but it was very brackish and most unpleasant to drink. Cupid struggled to swallow this foul-smelling liquid, but like her companions, her thirst was too severe and she had to make the best of it.

The Brigade remained at Romani for five days in order to rest, but the scene that greeted Cupid on her first morning on the outskirts of this small town was horrific. It took her mind back to those hideous days in the mud of northern France during the winter of 1915. Six months earlier, on the 4th and 5th of August 1916, Romani had been the scene of a very stiff battle.

Cupid and Vernon were returning from the wells at Katib Gannet. She still tasted the bitter water in her mouth and as she chomped on her bit, a string of slimy drool hung from her lips.

The strong north-westerly winds that blew in from the sea had blown the sand away from the shallow graves of hundreds of men, horses and camels, whose dead bodies had been hastily buried after the battle. Stray dogs were scratching about amongst these gruesome remains, scaring away the opportunistic vultures whose wings flapped lazily as they flew up into the remains of the few date-palm trees that had survived the battle and stood dotted about the battlefield in a bedraggled state.

Cupid's heart sank as she stood with Vernon on her back

surveying this revolting scene. Vernon kicked her on gently and they meandered slowly through the awful remains and back to the horse lines.

The five days of so-called rest for the men had turned into five days of horror. The horses watched as groups of men were formed into burial parties, and the partly-decomposed remains of the unfortunate men from both sides who had lost their lives in the battle were reinterred. A sombre air hung over these men as they dug relentlessly in the soft sand. The men streamed with sweat as they worked, and great clouds of flies swarmed about them, sticking to their drenched bodies. Cupid watched from the horse lines. The bitter taste in her mouth from the well water seemed to make her more thirsty. The ghastly smells from the hideous wasteland that lay before them made the horses nervous; they hated this more than anything. Horses are peaceful animals and would choose to play no part in such a revolting situation.

Since leaving their quiet homes in south Essex some two and a half years before, the horses and men had travelled some 3,800 miles through England, France and North Africa; most of these horses in a normal world would have travelled no further than a long day's hunting or a slow journey around the local villages delivering beer to the pubs, or pulling a plough, a harrow or a milk float. The men were local boys, and many had travelled no further than London or perhaps Southend-on-Sea, on a balmy summer's day. They had joined their local Batteries as peace-time Territorial soldiers, happy to spend two weeks a year on summer camp in far away places such as Lydd in Kent, to practice with their ancient guns, but were always home before the harvest began and back with their families. How could they ever have imagined the sort of scene that they were now part of in the hot sandy wastes of the Sinai desert? They might just as well have been transported to a different and extremely unpleasant planet.

On 10th February they left Romani. Cupid was glad to see the back of this awful place and was pleased to be moving again.

The Brigade now had about a hundred camels with it to carry food and water for the men; as before, each day's march was dictated by the distance to the next freshwater wells, which remained the only drinking water for the horses, who eventually became more used to this foul-smelling brackish liquid, such was their thirst after a long, hard day's work. On many days, the going was such that a full day's march would only cover a distance of perhaps eight or ten miles at the most. Then, when the wretched horses arrived at the wells in desperate need of water, the wooden troughs which were carried by the camels had to be erected and then filled by the men using canvas buckets. It was a long and arduous task which was often not completed until it was pitch dark.

The weather during February in this part of the world became more unpredictable and on some nights, just before dark, after the searing heat of the day, the heavens would open and torrents of rain would fall in a very short space of time, drenching everything. This made the watering operations even more difficult; the soaking men would stumble about in the half-light desperately trying to finish their work before they too could be fed and watered and then try and sleep in their now sodden blankets.

For the next twelve days the Brigade kept moving, stopping as usual at various outposts. They were following what was then known as the "Old Road" travelling east towards Palestine, the same road used by the retreating Turkish army after the battle of Romani. Littered beside the road were the decaying corpses of horses, camels, donkeys and mules, which in the humid conditions following the recent heavy rains swarmed with millions of disease-carrying flies. They swarmed around the horses' eyes and over their entire bodies, causing them to become unsettled and irritable. They also swarmed over the sweating bodies of the men with the same result. The stench of these rotting carcasses was overwhelming.

Cupid's eyes streamed. The grubby fly fringe that hung from her brow-band made no difference. Her whole body twitched and she thrashed her tail, trying to rid herself of the endless torment of the flies. Vernon on her back was equally restless; he fidgeted, flailed his arms in the air and cursed continuously.

On 15th February the Brigade arrived at Bir el Mazar. Here they stayed for a week of much-needed rest, the horses and men exhausted after their long march across such challenging country.

Cupid relished the chance to stand without a saddle on her back and be free to roll in the sand and shake. Vernon would groom her and talk quietly to her as he did so, and much to Cupid's surprise and delight, Bosche had reappeared as if from nowhere. He had been travelling on one of the wagons with Lordy the goose. Bosche also relished this short break, and lay in the sun beside Cupid, content that they were together again.

The next stage of their march began on 22nd February. El Arish was their destination and mercifully the going was firm. They were now travelling across salt pans, baked rock hard by the fierce sun, which allowed them to cover over ten miles each day, double the distance they had become used to whilst crossing the desert. The horses relished this hard going, but as ever the limited water supply dictated the length of the day's march.

The Brigade reached El Arish on the afternoon of the 24th February 1917 and would remain here until 20th March. El Arish had been captured from the Turks only two months earlier, and it was here that the enemy was seen again for the first time since leaving Suez at the beginning of January. German aeroplanes would circle in the distance, their observers peering through binoculars at the new arrivals with great interest. They never came close enough to cause any concern, but it was a reminder to all that the enemy was not far away.

Whilst at El Arish the Brigade camped along the coast, and on the first morning the men took the horses down to the sea, where they rode them bare-backed in the crashing waves. This was a delight to both man and beast. Cupid and Vernon galloped through the surf. After all that time in the desert it was exhilarating. They were of course joined by Flashlight, Polly and Bosche. Much to everybody's pleasure, the swimming became an almost daily routine. It was good for morale and beneficial to the health of both the horses and the men.

CHAPTER EIGHT

After nearly a month at El Arish, much rested and refurbished, the Brigade moved on again, arriving at Rafa on 24th March. Rafa was the frontier dividing Egypt and Palestine, and it was also, as if a line had been drawn into the earth, where the desert ended and the cultivated lands of southern Palestine began.

As suddenly as if entering another world, they found themselves marching across a grassy plain, not dissimilar to Salisbury Plain, where they had been so long ago, before leaving England to practise with their new guns. Dotted about them were bright green fields of barley, and the air was heavy with the delicious smells of wild flowers.

After so many weeks marching across the desert under the glaring heat of the sun and squinting day after day at the monotonous sandy landscape, the relief to the eyes from looking at a green and undulating country was remarkable, and in a strange way, incredibly restful.

Cupid looked about at this peaceful landscape; she could see sheep and goats grazing, and here and there a few cows, some lying contentedly chewing the cud, others standing in the shade of what seemed to be giant cactus hedges that acted as field boundaries, gently flicking their tails at the flies, which had unfortunately not diminished since leaving the desert. For the first time in weeks she heard birdsong. Beautifully coloured birds such as hoopoes and bee-eaters flitted here and there and small lizards scuttled through the grass in front of her as she and Vernon took in this extraordinary landscape.

Very early on the morning of 25th March, under the light of a brilliant moon, the march began again. It was a very cold morning and everything had become drenched by a heavy dew. The men and the horses longed for the sun to rise and to feel its warmth on their backs as they trudged on in the half light.

At about nine o'clock they arrived at a place called Bene Sala, where they were to rest for several hours. Cupid's spirits were lifted, the sun was now up and soon dried what was left of last night's dew. She looked about at the green and cultivated landscape. It had been many months since she had seen anything so beautiful. It was wonderful to hear the birdsong, and the air was filled with the smell of fresh green vegetation. There seemed to be a wonderfully relaxed mood that quickly spread throughout the Brigade.

Shortly after their arrival all the horses were unharnessed and turned out into a field of green barley. At first Cupid seemed to have forgotten what to do as she took her first few timid steps onto the soft carpet of green. Then she put her head down and began to graze; the young barley was succulent and delicious. Perhaps the farmer who had planted the barley would not have been so pleased, but to the seven hundred or so horses that now grazed to their heart's content it was a sublime pleasure.

A gentle breeze that blew in from the Mediterranean Sea kept the flies at least at a bearable level, and the air cooler.

The men also relaxed and sat in the shade of the giant cactus hedge that surrounded the barley field. They smoked, chatted and wrote letters home.

Vernon and Bosche sat in the shade watching this peaceful scene. Cupid grazed eagerly, on the sweet tender shoots of barley – not since leaving England had she or any of the other horses been treated to such a luxury. It was a much-needed and well-earned treat that ended abruptly that same afternoon.

By four o'clock the horses had been brought in from the barley field and before long they were harnessed up, hooked in and ready to move. In the cooler air of the early evening the Brigade crossed over some low hills and down onto a grassy plain, where for the first time, they could see the pretty town of Gaza, its white buildings shimmering in the light of the setting sun with the sparkling Mediterranean Sea behind. It was a scene as peaceful as anyone could wish for in a world torn apart by the ravages of war.

As the Brigade came down onto the plane, they could see columns of infantry, thousands strong, converging onto the small town of Deir el Belah, some eight miles south of Gaza. Here, owing to the plentiful supply of water, was the place where they would rest for the night.

It was dark before Cupid and her Brigade reached the place where they too would rest, sheltered in the hills that rose up to form the Goz el Taire Ridge.

It was to be a very short night, for by two o'clock in the morning of 26th March they were marching again. Up over the ridge they went, towards Gaza, heading for the south-eastern side of the town; they then descended into the deep dry bed of the Wadi Ghuzze, a huge dry water course carved out by the heavy rains of winter. The country around Gaza was ridden with these dry wadis. In the weeks to come their steep banks would provide excellent cover from the enemy artillery.

Very slow progress was made that morning, for suddenly, like an October morning in England, a thick white fog descended. Visibility was reduced to just a few yards and a strange muffled silence seemed to envelope the world.

This silence was not to last, for as the sun rose and burnt away the fog, the battle began. The guns opened up and the infantry began their attack on the Turkish outposts surrounding the town.

Cupid and her Brigade were at this early stage being held in reserve, and from their position they could hear the horrendous noise of battle as thousands of men charged forward behind a relentless artillery barrage.

The high command had fully expected this first assault on the town to be an easy affair, and serious opposition from the enemy had not been much considered; how wrong they had been. The enemy stuck to their positions like glue. Their artillery returned fire, and their machine-guns chattered relentlessly; a vicious battle raged and the casualties mounted.

Vernon sat silently on Cupid's back as they waited, listening and watching as the battle developed, their hearts pounding.

The sun was now high in the sky and the men sweltered under its powerful rays, their mouths going dry and the sweat streaming down their faces. The horses had not been watered since the previous evening and they too were suffering desperately from thirst in the intense heat. Cupid's sides heaved as her breathing became quicker. Vernon spoke quietly to her, patted her, and leaned forward in his saddle to gently stroke her ears.

The Brigade remained in reserve as the battle raged on, all three Batteries drawn up in line awaiting orders. As they waited under cover, hidden from the Turkish positions by the hills that formed Mansura Ridge, enemy aircraft became very active and soon their position was given away. An enemy artillery battery opened fire on them and suddenly the air was filled with bursting shells. Some of the horses panicked. The men desperately tried to calm them and hold them steady, but several horses were wounded as they tried to move back from the terrifying onslaught. By some miracle only one man was wounded.

The battle became more and more intense, and the infantry attacked again and again, the casualties mounting. Eventually, about mid-afternoon, the reserves were ordered into action. Crossing the Mansura Ridge, the Brigade formed a line and came into action in the open, their twelve 18-pounder guns firing over open sights directly at the enemy as the infantry charged in behind the barrage with bayonets fixed.

Out in the open as they were, they presented an easy target for the enemy guns. An enemy aircraft circled over them dropping smoke bombs to create a better target for its artillery, but their shooting was poor and the shells burst harmlessly in front of them. The smoke only made it more difficult for the Brigade's gunners to see their targets; many hundreds of rounds were expended that afternoon until finally when the sun set, a cease-fire was ordered and the Brigade withdrew to a place called El Burjaliye, where they would spend the hours of darkness in a cornfield. The horses remained harnessed up and the spent ammunition was replaced. There was to be no rest for either man or beast that night and more importantly, no water.

The men and horses worked all night. The men drained their water bottles, some offering a dribble to their wretched horses, but these tiny amounts would make no difference.

By the next morning Cupid and all the other horses were craving water. They were reluctant to work, and all that the tired men could do was to coax them on.

The Brigade was in action again all the next day. Thousands more rounds of ammunition were used and it was not until dusk that the army finally withdrew and the first battle of Gaza was over.

The 26th and 27th March 1917 had been exhausting for both man and beast and it wasn't until late in the afternoon on the 27th that the camels carrying the water eventually arrived. The column had been shelled on their approach, greatly limiting the supply. The horses had not been watered for over 24 hours and were utterly exhausted. Slowly, in the dark they made their way back to Deir el Belah, which they reached by 04.30 in the morning of 28th March. The horses' stumbling on the uneven ground kept the men from sleeping in their saddles throughout the painful journey.

The next fortnight was spent recuperating; during which time Vernon and his father wrote letters home. His father wrote a few short lines on 30th March:

We are all well. Practically no serious casualty in the Bde, which did splendidly. We've all been done to a turn – thirst – dust & want of sleep. Everybody has been splendid. We are in cultivated land. I dare write nothing more.

He wrote again on 2nd April:

I am writing this in my little bivvy by the aid of a flickering dip – very cramped & uncomfortable – but full of bully beef & (for a great treat) some bread. You will have guessed we have had a great battle, I wrote you a line after to say all was well, I cannot of course give you any details. The battle lasted 2 days & one night & as we had no sleep for 2 nights before it or the night after it you will understand that it was exhausting, thirst & absence of sleep are very trying but we are all as fit as fiddles now. Old Flashlight was so tired that he sat down under me, just to rest. Bosche turned up after the battle from goodness knows where, he is a wonder. I am dirty and flea bitten, but fit.

On 5th April Vernon wrote:

A very long gap since my last letter. We had two day's fighting during which we had one topping afternoons shooting, we were extraordinarily lucky in not being shelled at all when in action and during the 2 days we only had one man wounded and 1 horse killed in the whole brigade. We had a pretty thirsty time of it during the two days and our horses were only watered twice, but all managed to survive all right. My little dog stayed behind with the transport and I found him again the day after the battle. We are at present resting & we hope, waiting for another battle as the Turk is not far away.

We are now right clear of the desert which is ripping, the country is just like Salisbury Plain and all cultivated, the horses are piqueted in a barley field which is rather nice for them. There are any amount of lizards and tortoises about and some ripping birds 'Hoo Poos" and Bea-eaters besides the ordinary sheep and cows which are pleasant sights after the desert.

The horses were again allowed to graze freely in the barley fields, but this was not to last long. There were so many thousands of horses competing for this luxury that the fields were soon nothing but dry stalks and the air was full of dust as they scraped with their hooves to find the last remnants of what had once been so delicious.

They shared their grazing with horses from every other unit in the vicinity, many of them from the Australian cavalry. The men got on well with the Australians; they shared their rations with them, listened to stories and sang songs with them. They had a common bond, which was their love of their horses, particularly the Australian Walers which had served them so well since they left Marseille all that time before. Vernon's father says in one of his letters:

I like the Australians, such fighters, such good cavalry. This is a great sight here, so much cavalry, so many horses...

The days were very hot, but the nights were perishing cold. Cupid found it hard to acclimatise to these strange conditions. She loved the sun on her back during the day but the nights were very trying. Luckily there was a plentiful supply of water from the wells at Deir el Belah and the horses were rather left to their own devices during this fortnight of rest; the men were busy preparing for the second battle of Gaza.

CHAPTER NINE

❧

On 16th April 1917 the Brigade was ordered to prepare to march at midnight to support an attack on the Sheikh Abbas Ridge which was to begin at dawn.

For the first time they were accompanied by tanks. The horses were appalled by the sight and sound of these huge machines. The roar of the engines, the clouds of exhaust fumes that filled the air and the showers of sparks that flew out from behind them as they lumbered over the uneven ground in the dark were terrifying, and the men had to work hard to calm them.

When the attack began in the half light of dawn, the noise was cacophonic and the flashes and bangs of the explosions were truly awesome. One of the tanks suffered a direct hit from the enemy artillery and blew up, an horrific sight.

Cupid thought yet again that the world was ending. The noise was so terrible and the air was so full of flying metal that all she could do was rely on Vernon to guide her and encourage her, though he too was wondering about their chances of survival in this hellish place.

The battle raged on all day and the next night, when under the cover of darkness the Brigade advanced further towards the enemy trenches. It opened fire again at first light, and during the next two hours over three thousand rounds of ammunition were hurled at the enemy.

Cupid was exhausted. She was dying of thirst and felt as if her head would burst. The noise was so intense that she could hear nothing. How she longed to escape this nightmare! Should she just bolt – gallop away as fast as she could? Surely there must be a way out? There was of course no escape, and any attempt to do so would probably have been fatal. The men coaxed their horses on and somehow between them they survived until darkness fell.

The second attempt by the British to take Gaza had also failed, though some useful ground had been gained. The Turks still occupied the town itself and both armies now settled down to a long period of trench warfare. The guns were dug in and mercifully for the horses, they were sent back behind to the wagon lines, where for the foreseeable future they would be in less danger.

Cupid, Polly and Flashlight arrived back at the wagon lines in a sorry state. Over the last few days of the battle they had had very little water and even less food. They had frozen at night and sweltered under the relentless rays of the sun during the day. They had been tormented by the clouds of flies that feasted on the rotting remains of the dead men and horses that littered the battlefield.

Shortly afterwards Vernon also appeared, in an equally sorry state.

On 30th April 1917 his father wrote:

We started another battle 14 days ago & are still at it, dug in now of course, same old game. After the strenuous week of the second battle I saw the boy was getting worn and strung up so I sent him back to the Depot and had a fresh officer up for a while, so he, Cupid and Bosche are taking a rest. I am as fit as a fiddle, though I suffer from sore feet, never taking my boots off, thirst dirt & funk of high explosive shells. I got very thin, having to tear about with the infantry, giving them close support, getting no sleep & little food, but now I am in a dug out with at least sufficient food & irregularities more regular. I am up by the front line, no horse near, my guns behind me, and a bewildering number of Turks in front of me. It is a lovely rolling cultivated open country, barley just ripening, no roads, no houses or villages, with the pretty city of Gaza & the Mediterranean smiling before us. The weather hot by day but very cold early morning, pleasant at times & occasional showers, but the hot dusty Khamsin wind is awful and one dies of thirst on a gallon of chlorinated warm water per person. I have a dear little Egyptian Army Bivouac tent, but that is no good against shell fire, so I have to burrow now. It is now growing dark 6.50 pm & the bore is one cannot have a light – even if lights were procurable. There is a canteen some miles back and we now get a camel or pack horse to come along with some tinned fruit or biscuits etc. I cannot see to write anymore now.

Best love.

On 3rd May, Vernon wrote:

At the moment of writing I am at the base with my old section which is the depot. Dads sent me down here because I was not very fit for a bit of a rest and then I think someone else will have a turn.

The Turk is a very hard and stubborn fighter and has stood up well against superior numbers and equipment. They seem short of personal equipment as they rob our dead and even the wounded of almost everything they possess.

I was lucky in being able to bring my two horses down for a rest besides myself, they wanted it badly too. Little Bosche, I think you have seen pictures of him, was with the transport during the two battles and joined us in between.

The men were suffering from the intense heat and the shortage of drinking water, and from aching heads due to the continuous gunfire. They took it in turns to be rested, and the relief at being away from the horrors of the front must have been extraordinary.

For the horses, being back at the wagon lines was a life saver. For the first time in days their feed and water was regular, and to be out of harness and nurtured by the men was a huge comfort. Many of the horses had suffered wounds, which became easily infected in this fly-blown country, and the vets worked tirelessly with the men to make them more comfortable.

Luckily for Cupid, she had escaped unhurt, but she was thin and exhausted. The little mare from Essex whose life had once been so perfect stood amongst her friends confused and bewildered in this strange and unforgiving world.

On 24th May Vernon wrote again:

I have re-joined the Battery and have been back about a week now feeling as fit as a fiddle and very pleased to be back with my pals again. My horses are with me, much rested and improved, also little Bosche.

All the horses have improved tremendously since I left, it is a funny thing that horses don't get their summer coats any earlier here than in England, but their old coats die on them so that they go that horrid yellow colour that horses always go just as they are changing their coats, in about March.

Our life now consists of 3 kinds of existence. First living at the observing post with the Infantry which is pretty uncomfortable though my turn has not come yet, secondly living at the guns which is more comfortable, and is where I am at present, and thirdly living at the wagon line with the horses and wagons which is the most comfortable of all as it is possible to erect a small bivouac tent, also more water is available. Little Bosche has to live there, as he is 'gun shy'. He lives with three other dogs and a goose, the battery pets!

How horrible for the horses to have their winter coats hanging off them amongst the flies and the dirt and the other nastinesses of warfare, but at least their general condition had improved.

Also good news to hear from this letter that Lordy the goose had survived all this time. Perhaps she had been laying some tasty eggs to supplement the army rations, but most probably she was just a friendly pet, lovingly looked after by the men to help take their minds back to those carefree days before the war when the ponds in the farmyards or on the village green had been home to ducks and geese, and where many a summer's evening had been spent, perhaps with a pint of beer outside the pub with a wife or girlfriend, watching the children throwing bread or other leftovers for the birds to feed on.

The Brigade remained in action throughout the summer of 1917. The weather became hotter and hotter, the countryside dried up and any movement caused clouds of dust to rise into the air;

fortunately for the horses, the water supply to the wagon lines remained constant and the newly built railway had now reached them, which meant that forage was also plentiful. The barley fields that had provided such delicious grazing just those few weeks earlier had now vanished and were little more than dust bowls.

Cupid, Polly and Flashlight regained their strength and the men came and went as they took their turns to rest. It was always a relief when Vernon reappeared at the wagon lines after a turn at the front. The first thing he would do when he arrived would be to find Cupid and Bosche. They were of course well looked after by the other men, but life just seemed a little more normal when they were together.

All day long they could hear the guns booming and see in the distance the clouds of smoke and dust rising into the air. At night, sometimes when the guns were not firing, it seemed almost eerily quiet; crickets could be heard, and the strange nocturnal noises and calls of other animals as they scuttled about their business. How strange and comforting that the animal world carries on as normal while human beings do their utmost to destroy each other.

Here are extracts from the letters that Vernon and his father wrote home during this period of trench warfare. They rarely miss mentioning the horses or their wellbeing, and frequently tell of the birds and animals they encounter in their day-to-day lives. Their thoughts are also of home.

On 4th June 1917, Vernon's father writes:

I wonder if you will be eating green peas by the time this reaches you. I think you will be well advised not to try and make hay too early, when it is very sappy it takes longer to make. By the end of the first week in July it should take very little making if the weather is hot, and it will have done growing. The bottom land is generally better for being left till mid July.

I cannot help thinking this war is drawing to a close, but I suppose the wish is father to the thought. The Turks are pretty sick of it, they have to patrol the front of their line to stop men deserting over to our lines, but almost every night one or two manage to get across. Yet in defence they are such wonderful fighters. They have dug themselves in very deep, and never show themselves within range of gunfire.

All our trenches, communication trenches, redoubts etc. made here by the Essex Brigade have Essex names, Ongar Road, Chelmsford Road, Boreham Cock, Barking etc. etc.

I have had quite a lot of riding these last few days and it has been very hot at midday.

On 9th June 1917 Vernon writes:

Life is not at all bad at present, of course it is very hot, but not unbearable, the worst hardship is the flies, though just now we have a dugout which is moderately clear of them. At the moment I am at the battery observing station, among the Infantry, and am having quite good fun potting at the Turk when he appears above ground and in range, which is not very often just now. At present he is getting on our particular part of the line 10 times as many shells as he sends over.

I had a splendid rest at the base and am now feeling fitter than I have ever done out here. The country, although it makes awful dust and has gone very brown, still has green patches in it and quite a lot of small birds – a water wagtail has a nest in one of the trenches here!

The insects and small reptiles are extremely numerous and various. One thing I forgot to tell you about the second battle was the 'tanks' you will have heard about them in France. I hope someday to be able to get inside one.

Little Bosche has been either wounded or bitten during two days absence from the Battery, I have not seen him for about a fortnight as he has to stay in the wagon line when I am with the guns or at the O.P. he is very gun shy!

Bosche recovered from his wounds and life continued, the horses being used when needed, and the men taking turns to be up at the front or resting at the wagon lines with the horses.

Some time during the middle of June, Vernon went into hospital suffering from diphtheria, to stay for several weeks. There was a good deal of illness amongst the men during the summer of 1917. Sandfly fever was rife and any kind of open sore or wound would soon turn septic, thanks to the swarms of disease-carrying flies that were a constant torment.

On 26th June the Vernon's father writes again:

I am now in a different part of the line, and have excavated in the sides of a Wadi another little sand bagged village for my Hd Qtrs.......... I don't think we get shelled so much here as in the last place but in other respects I like it less, there are more fleas and it is dirty, and I have a very long walk to the trenches, and there are rifle and machine gun bullets to contend with, but it is nearer the sea and there is more breeze. At the other place we had a succession of really pretty wild flowers, wild thyme which scented the whole air, but I also had in my dug out there 2 tarantulas, most awful brutes, they are spiders as big as crabs, with fat podgy bodies like toads, & mouths like sharks. It has been very hot lately, unbearable between 12 & 4 o'clock but the heat comes and goes in waves. I defend myself against fleas and bugs by rubbing your citronella over my hands, arms & face at night, and they tell me the whole Wadi smells of it.

At present Vernon is in hospital with Diphtheria, a mild form I believe and hope. It is of course like him to go and catch anything that is knocking about. Everybody has something wrong lately, I have just recovered from a streaming cold, running at the eyes & nose, most unpleasant in a blazing sun.

Tell my mother that the making of Hospital requisites is good work. After our two battles here we ran short of medical stores like bandages etc. and one realised what an enormous consumption there is, especially when ship loads of everything get sunk. When the Turk shells my line I retaliate 10 fold immediately, he knows just what to expect each time he opens on us. We have air photographs to show us where he lives etc. & then we pump them into him. It is no good making war with kid gloves.

CHAPTER TEN

❦

At last, during the first week of August the Brigade was withdrawn from the line and relieved by another. Over two days, 4th and 5th August, the horses, guns, wagons and all other equipment were taken back to a rest camp near Deir el Belah; they were bivouacked in the fig groves on the edge of the town, near the sand dunes of Sheikh Shabassi.

The guns were hidden amongst the fig trees and camouflaged to hide them from enemy aeroplanes.

It was a relief to all to be out of the line, but the rest camp was a beastly, dirty place; the sand dunes sheltered the camp from the sea breeze, making the intense heat of the sun during the day almost unbearable. The place swarmed with clouds of flies and was infested with fleas.

Worst of all for the horses were the camel ticks. These hard-cased parasites were vicious and would grow to the size of a thumbnail, gorging themselves on the blood of their victim.

The only advantage for the horses was the closeness of the camp to the sea. Twice a day, in the early morning and evening when the sun was not so hot, they would be taken to the beach where, as before at El Arish, they would be ridden bareback through the crashing waves.

Cupid longed for the time spent at the beach, as did Vernon and Bosche; the salt water allowed a temporary relief from the ticks and flies and fleas.

It was a great sight, hundreds of men and horses converging onto the beach to mingle with men from other units who were also resting; there were British troops, Australians and Indians, all enjoying this temporary relief from the front line. Friendships were made, stories told and rations shared. There were also a good deal of friendly, but none the less fiercely competitive, displays of horsemanship.

This short period of rest was soon over and on 23rd and 24th August the Brigade was returned to the line, back to their old positions at Kurd Hill, along what was known as Happy Valley. Although the rest had been in many respects beneficial to all, the unhealthy conditions of the campsite in the fig grove were causing problems amongst the men; many began to suffer from sceptic sores, boils and other unpleasant conditions and sandfly fever was again rife amongst them.

At the beginning of September Vernon is in hospital again, this time with sandfly fever. On 4th September he writes:

Here I am in hospital again which is very annoying, rotten fever this time, the result I am afraid of living in a plantation of fig trees which made the place awfully damp and unhealthy, several men went down with the same complaint. We had a fortnights rest as a Division and we were arranging some rather good Battery sports when we were suddenly ordered back into the line again.

Someday we will have another fight out here I expect, but I expect they will wait till it is a bit cooler.

There are simply thousands of lizards in Palestine just now, little Bosche has great fun chasing them he is rather rough and breaks off their tails, which is a nuisance.

My horses were very well when I left, I still have 22 left who marched away from Essex out of 60 odd, which is not bad.

As summer turned to autumn and the days grew shorter, the cooler weather that was expected failed to materialise. The stalemate of trench warfare continued and the guns from both sides continued to bombard one another, day after day.

By the beginning of October the air had become sticky, the rains had not yet arrived and the humid heat was awful for the horses, which were by now growing their winter coats. Any work they had to do became twice as difficult, and for the same reason the men became grumpy.

On 14th October the Brigade was relieved again and withdrew back to the rest area amongst the fig trees at Deir el Belah; sadly for the men, 'rest' was the one thing that they were not going to do much of during these few days away from the line. It was here that they were to prepare themselves for the forthcoming third attack on Gaza.

Cupid, Flashlight and Polly were together in the horse lines, but sadly there was to be no bathing in the sea this time. The horses were groomed and vetted to ensure they were fit for action. The saddlers and farriers were hard at work and there was a permanent background noise of ringing anvils as the men worked.

All day and night new troops were arriving, and new equipment; for the first time Cupid saw a Battery of heavy guns and Howitzers being drawn towards the front by gun tractors, huge machines on tracks, just like the tanks, squealing and rattling along, belching out great plumes of black, oily smoke.

Between 21st and 24th October they began to move towards their new positions on the left flank of the line, close to Sheikh Ajlin and very near to the sea amongst the sand dunes.

During the night of 26-27 October a huge thunderstorm erupted over them. The whole sky was lit up with continuous lightning and the rumbling thunder was so loud that it obliterated the noise of the artillery from both sides; the rain was torrential and everything was drenched. This was the first real rain that Cupid had felt on her back since February. At first she liked it, as the smell of the wet earth after such a long period of dry heat was a reminder of happier days, but the feeling soon passed. The crashing thunder and lightning were frightening, and the sodden men became bad-tempered as they tried to work in the flooded gun-pits and dug-outs. It was a long and trying night.

The sky had cleared by the morning of Saturday 27 October, and at first light the bombardment of Gaza began; it was to continue day and night for the next eleven days. Tens of thousands of rounds of ammunition were used. It was exhausting work for the men and horses that were constantly re-supplying the guns. Over the next few days the infantry attacked and attacked and the enemy fought back, both sides pounding each other with artillery.

On 30 October, the Royal Navy arrived just off the coast. HMS *Grafton*, two gunboats, two destroyers and four monitors, some with huge 14-inch guns, began to bombard Gaza from the sea. The noise was simply incredible.

In the early hours of 7 November 1917, Gaza was finally taken.

It had been an horrendous and costly battle on both sides. The horses had been worked to the bone. For the last five days of the battle the horses had been kept harnessed up day and night in readiness to move, and those bringing fresh ammunition up to the guns had worked non stop. Forage and water had been in very limited supply throughout the battle and it was a wonder how the horses coped under these conditions.

On 9th November Vernon's father writes:

I suppose I can write now. We've had a top-hole battle, a real big one - and we've had a real victory. We bombarded the enemy relentlessly for 6 days and 5 nights incessantly, and then on the 6th night we went for him. We took all of his first line & some of his second line defences, and then for 6 more days we had to hammer and fight day & night, he fought like a dog at bay and continuously counter attacked. On our right the Cavalry took Beersheba and progressed splendidly. On the 12th night he hooked it, and did a wonderful evacuation. At 9 o'clock at night he was fighting in his trenches, at 1 a.m. we gave him an intense bombardment & rushed some works and found him gone! At day break I was 4 ½ miles over the heavy sand after him with my own 2 Batteries shooting the remnants of his transport and straggling troops. I and my 2 Batteries were the first guns to be ordered to move in pursuit. We cannot now go further for want of water, roads & Ry, but the Cavalry are round him, and his Palestine Army is destroyed. By God's providence I had very few casualties in my own two Batteries, and in my group of 6 we came off very lightly.

I am now in my Bivvy on a breezy cliff a few miles N of Gaza. The battlefield is disgusting but interesting, I've just been riding over it. I have had very little sleep for ten days or so, but a battle is very exhilarating.

I have the profoundest admiration for the Turkish soldier, what he has stood is incredible. He is game to the last, and with a machine gun in a battered trench or a hole in the ground he is a devil to dislodge.

We've collard stacks of German made war material & ammunition.

He writes again on 12th November:

I am writing this in my Bivvy which is flapping about in a hurricane of wind & dust. It is most uncomfortable, but better than everlasting shell fire. The battle has been a great success, we've got at present over 70 of his guns and about 6000 prisoners, and judging by what I have seen we have killed a great number. We turned both his flanks in the battle, the Cavalry got behind him, and it really has been a great show. We are very proud of our C in C. I commanded the Artillery on the extreme left, and our Infantry had to capture his right flank defences & hold them until we could force him out of his main defences by threatening his rear & bombarding his position until it was untenable. You never saw such a mess as our guns have made of all his works & Battery positions etc. when I advanced my own two Batteries I came along the sea shore and the Infantry cheered the Batteries. Our Army has pushed on a long way but our Division is resting from its labours and lending all its transport to help others on. Yesterday I revisited the ground where we fought on March 26th and actually buried some of our Essex men who fell that day. It has been continuous fighting ever since then.

My horses are all splendidly well, and they have had hard work pulling up so many thousands of rounds of ammunition to the guns over heavy sand. Old Flashlight bears himself with great pride, Polly & Cupid perennially young, and Bosche has reappeared from the back area.

Vernon also writes home on 12th November:

It has been a splendid show, we had a great bombardment for six days, then attacked by night and after 4 days pretty stiff fighting the Turks retired, and they have been well harassed for the last few days during their retreat.

I have had the most awfully interesting time riding round Gaza and seeing all the Turk gun positions and trenches which we have been shooting at so long. He left any amount of ammunition of all kinds. His Infantry fought most gallantly before they retired and he lost very heavily indeed, I rode round some trenches 2 days after he evacuated and they were covered with dead, a beastly sight. There was an extraordinary lack of secure dugouts unlike the German cement & concrete pits, and all his gun positions had shell holes all round them, which speaks well for our heavy artillery work.

Our horses are rather pulled down by excessive work, we are very busy carting ammunition just at present which is hard work especially as we have not been able to get their heavy coats off yet owing to lack of clippers.

I sent little Bosche to a dump of surplus kit for the battle, he stayed there for about 10 days, and then apparently when the battle subsided he went off to look for us and was found by Dads trekking off with a Brigade which relieved us in our last position, he had evidently gone back there to find us.

The weather is ripping just now and the country is beginning to get green again, we had an awful thunder- storm the other night and all got absolutely soaked.

Cupid was completely worn out. She had been worked to the bone; she had had a saddle on her back twenty-four hours a day, for nearly a fortnight. Her long shaggy coat was driving her mad. She had been dreadfully hot and so thirsty and the continuous noise of the battle rang in her ears. She had loathed her ride over the battlefield, where the stench and the flies were indescribable; the corpses and mangled remains of men, horses and mules that lay amongst the wreckage were disgusting. Several of her friends had been killed during the battle and many more wounded.

The only redeeming feature of this nightmare had been the gentle kindness of the men; they too were utterly exhausted, but every spare minute that they had was given up for the horses.

CHAPTER ELEVEN

❧

There was to be very little rest for either man or beast for the remainder of 1917 as they chased the Turkish Army relentlessly northward. The going was very hard on the horses, as eight horse teams were needed to pull the guns through the deep sand and teams of six or eight horses were needed to pull the heavily-laden ammunition wagons and general service wagons.

The weather remained very hot by day, and still the horses had not been clipped. All along their route lay the hideous remains of warfare; unburied corpses, dead horses and mules and wrecked equipment. Stray dogs scavenged amongst the remains and birds pecked at the rotting flesh, searching for maggots. The flies swarmed over everything in vast clouds.

By the beginning of December, they had moved further inland and into cultivated country. Gone was the deep, soft sand; this was rich fertile, clay soil, baked hard by the sun, out of which grew orange, olive and almond trees. A few houses were dotted amongst the orange groves and there were one or two small villages still occupied, mainly by women and children.

Ripe oranges still hung from the trees; there was no market for them, and not enough manpower to harvest them even if there had been a market. It was however possible for the men to buy small amounts from the locals to supplement their rations.

On 5th December Vernon writes:

The country here is lovely, rather brown and dry at present, but lots of lovely Jaffa oranges to eat and things like that. The hills (Judaea) are awfully pretty morning and evening and are very similar to the hills near the canal.

There are several Jewish settlements and German settlements too, they farm under modern conditions and supply us with a little fresh meat, eggs, butter, jam and honey they can only give us small quantities, but of course only a little of these luxuries are a tremendous boon while campaigning!

There is one German colony right in our front line and the inhabitants and their livestock are still living there. I went there yesterday to buy some food and found two wretched girls in one house where we bought butter, very frightened and many women and children in the other houses, many of which have been hit by shells. Of course they could clear out, and they are Huns, but one cannot help admiring their pluck and being sorry for them, in spite of what they have done to France.

No doubt an even distribution of such distress will bring home to all countries in time the frightfulness of war when it affects peoples' homes and women & children.

Little Bosche is still with me & goes everywhere except the actual front line & I only stop him from coming there, as he would attract too much attention.

We are at present awaiting the rainy season, we have had only 3 days this winter and so there is a lot overdue which will be very

*unpleasant when it does come. All the Wadis (dry rivers) will come
down and make things very unpleasant for everyone!*

Vernon was correct with his forecast; after days of struggling
through the deep sand, it was a merciful relief to be traveling over
a hard surface again through this pretty country, even though the
enemy was only a few miles in front of them.

Within days of them reaching this easy-going terrain, huge
black clouds rolled in, the sun disappeared, the temperature
plummeted and the rainy season began. Day after day the rain fell
in torrents. The hard clay surface that had offered such relief to
the struggling horses was quickly turned into a quagmire and the
dry wadis were soon flowing like rivers in spate. The going became
almost impossible; the horses slipped and fell, wagons turned over
and guns were stuck axle-deep. The landscape became more like
Flanders than Palestine.

The camels that were carrying the forage for the horses and
rations for the men were unable to move at all across the sucking
clay. These wonderful creatures that had worked so hard for so
long were not designed for conditions like this; they became stuck
in the glutinous, oozing mud, their huge loads still strapped onto
their backs.

The whole country became almost impassable; the men
suffered from the sudden drop in temperature as they were still
dressed in their thin khaki. Their bivouacs collapsed under the
heavy weight of water and rations and forage were lost in the mud
with no chance of any new supplies being brought up.

Some of the men were able to shelter in the empty houses, but
they were so few and far between that most had to shiver under
their flapping canvas bivouacs.

The men and horses were put on half rations; the men at least were able to supplement their ration of biscuits and everlasting bully beef with oranges that still hung from the trees. The wretched horses however were pitifully short of food, and would remain so until the skies cleared and transport became possible again. The few small luxuries that the men had been able to acquire from the locals were soon a distant memory.

The horses stood huddled in the horse lines, hock-deep in mud. Having endured months of searing heat, they felt chilled to the bone as the rain lashed down on their backs. The nights seemed endless, and they were so hungry; they stood hanging their heads, listening to the howling jackals and waiting for relief from this torture.

All this time the fighting continued and the strain upon the horses working in these conditions was enormous, as so much was expected of them. The army simply could not have operated without them; even the elaborate new gun tractors that Cupid had seen before the last battle of Gaza had become bogged belly-deep in the mud, their great weight rendering them quite useless.

By the end of the year they had crossed the Auja River, and on 22 and 23 December the attack on Mulebbis was prepared. Advancing the next day, the attack soon petered out, as the enemy had already evacuated the town.

Vernon's father writes on 26th December:

I have had various letters & newspapers to thank you for, and a few days ago when my bivouac was flooded out by torrential rain and we were nearly all drowned I had a parcel of sweets including some mint balls called 'a chilly man's fire' which met the situation well! I am eating one now sitting in a house with my greatcoat over my knees trying to keep warm, but it has drenched with rain for nearly a week & everything is damp, it is almost impossible to get warm. However it is something to be in a house! We are in a Jewish colony, we took it in the battle of the Auja river a few days ago, and we are surrounded by orange groves laden with fruit for which there is no market, olives, vines, almonds and fields of wheat etc. The people here have had no sugar for 2 years, have no meat, butter, milk or cheese, the Turk having lived on them and destroyed the place a good deal.

We are at the end of our tether with a roadless country behind us of deep soft clay completely waterlogged and we are on half rations and forage. We have had a lot of fighting to get this strong line but our last battle proved very easy as the Turk realised he was outgunned and soon hooked it.

We are not far from Gilgal and the whole country is teeming with interest, and also it is beautiful and fertile. It is certainly God's own country.

Vernon is very fit, and Bosche always turns up after battles, he either finds me or Vernon or one of the Batteries, & everybody knows him.

This has been a great campaign of infinite variety, and we have been fighting for 9 months continuously, after marching all the way from Egypt, and we have been dashed lucky.

CHAPTER TWELVE

✂

Mulebbis, not far from Jaffa, and the surrounding area was to be their home for the first three months of 1918; during the first week in January the rains finally ceased. Each day saw a little more sunshine and the temperature slowly lifted.

This was to be the first proper rest for the horses after nine months of continuous fighting, and as the weather improved, so did their spirits.

The countryside slowly became green again and in groups, a few at a time, the horses were turned out to graze on the fresh green shoots. While they waited for their turn to be let out, they were rested and as far as possible, pampered, and after all this time they were at last clipped; day after day the clipping machines rattled away, and at long last their dying, shaggy coats were removed.

The men became more cheerful as the weather improved. They were very near to the front line, and the enemy occasionally sent over a few shells and a few were fired back, but it was generally quiet.

Thousands of troops were gathering in the vicinity; the men renewed friendships with Australians and New Zealanders who they had met during the long preparations for the battles at Gaza.

The cooler weather since the rains made life much more comfortable for the horses and there were fewer flies, which was a huge relief, and a plentiful supply water and forage.

Whilst they were at the horse lines or at the watering troughs, the horses would watch the world go around; Cupid was fascinated by her surroundings. Since the rains had stopped local people had appeared as if from nowhere, with horses, donkeys and mules to carry on with their daily work; though it must be said that the animals that were put to work were generally not fit enough for the task. Any animal that had any real work left in it had been taken by the Turkish army.

The locals tried as much as possible to carry on with their normal lives, but the war had destroyed so much of their property and infrastructure that daily life was a struggle. They lived mainly off the land and were now trying to market their oranges, almonds and figs, also pitifully small amounts of wheat and barley, all threshed by hand, or rather by animals. In a letter home, Vernon describes the threshing process:

I have just taken some photographs, which I will send you copies of the threshing floors they have in the Arab villages here, it is the most primitive business you ever saw, the corn is laid out in a circular heap about 4 feet deep & then cows, donkeys or camels are driven round and round on it until the straw is reduced to chaff and the grain stamped out of the ear, I don't suppose it has changed a bit since the time of David and Solomon.

The donkeys and mules struggled under huge loads, bringing the fruit etc. to the hastily erected market place. Cupid watched the miserable creatures being goaded on by their owners. She could hear the shouting and the occasional thwack of a stick. She pitied the poor animals and so did the men, as they hated seeing animals treated this way, and it wasn't long before they intervened. They realised, of course, how much these people had suffered in recent times and how much the ravages of war had affected their livelihoods, but they couldn't simply sit back and watch these wretched animals suffer. The army vets helped as much as they could, the farriers cut the horribly overgrown hoofs on the donkeys and the men tried to persuade the owners not to overload their animals to such an extent. Translation was a problem and on many occasions, not surprisingly, they were told to mind their own business.

However, to a certain extent it did work; many of the local farmers were desperate to cultivate their ground, plough the stubble fields and attempt to establish a new crop. It was now early February and time was running out. The Turkish army having taken all their fit horses, they struggled with the few animals they had left.

It was decided by the commanding officers that horses would be lent to farmers by the day to help with the ploughing, one man to accompany each horse. Many of the draught horses had been farm horses before the war, and many of the men had also worked on the land. It was easy work for the horses, pulling an ancient single furrow plough, and a comforting distraction for the men that went with them. It took their minds away from army life, the front line and the war, and back to happier times in the peaceful Essex countryside.

During these first three months of 1918 Cupid's Brigade remained just behind the front line. Occasionally they would be sent forward into action to relieve other Batteries at the front, but mostly, as far as the horses were concerned, it was a reasonably quiet time, except for Cupid and Polly.

The General had been away for some weeks and while he was away Vernon's father had been made acting CRA (Commander Royal Artillery), which meant leaving the Brigade and living at Divisional Headquarters. Flashlight of course went with him, and from the second week in January so did Cupid and Polly. Vernon had gone away on leave, leaving his horses with his father, so the three old stable-mates were together again.

As usual, when not up at the front, the men soon found ways to entertain themselves; sporting competitions were arranged, football matches, concert parties and of course equestrian challenges.

After a long gap, a few mails began to arrive; letters and parcels from home were much looked forward to. On 1st March Vernon's father writes:

Parcels dribble in by slow degrees, but take about 3 months to do the journey. I have had the candles, and most welcome for we had to light ourselves with olive oil in a cigarette tin & a wick made of medical bandage. I have some parcels that I haven't opened yet because I am still at Divisional HdQtrs acting CRA, and am keeping my parcels until I get back to my own Brigade where the contents will be more welcome, for here I live in great comfort. The weather has been wintry, very wet at times & cold. I suffered greatly until I got up my thick clothes from Port Said, until about January 10th I was wearing the same clothes as during the summer, and had no waterproof, now I have everything. I am about 10 miles from the front line & as I ride to some part of it every day I get any amount of exercise. The going is good for riding & the horses very fit so riding is a pleasure. I don't know how people get on who don't like riding. We have been having steeple chases and sports behind the line, many football matches etc. I was rather pleased at winning the jumping competition at Divisional sports, out of 23 competitors all much junior & years younger than myself my horse went round the course without touching a twig!

The General is expected back any day now and I shall return to my Bde. I have only been with them about a fortnight ever since Nov 18th it has been rather a varied experience. The country is getting lovely now, but not nearly enough of it cultivated. The wild flowers are wonderful, wild sweet smelling geranium, great varieties of anemones or crocuses, and in the hills quantities of cyclamen, dear little dwarf bushes of gorse and broom and lots of little pink & blue flowers which give a sort of coloured sheen to large patches of ground. In the cultivated areas there are hundreds of acres of almond trees in full bloom, apricots, and orange groves with fruit still on them and blossom in bud. The people are poor, picturesque & smelly, the women carry everything on their heads and have a most stately walk, and are attractive looking in their trousers & robes and head covers of patchwork, their clothes are generations old, patched with every colour and pattern possible, and I expect never taken off.

By the time Vernon returned, some time during the last week in March, Cupid and Polly were fit and well. It seems they had had some interesting experiences as well. His father had been riding Cupid on 12th March and after a busy day, he writes home on 13th:

I am still acting General and yesterday we had a great battle, which was most successful and drew great praise upon the Artillery who though I say it, put up a real good show. The credit is not due to me but to our General who is himself a Gunner and devised the scheme. Our Batteries however had both difficult and dangerous tasks, and they were quite splendid. We had most extraordinary good luck in avoiding serious casualties and one cannot expect such luck always, but it was a ripping show. If one has got to be at war one might as well "have at it", but the end does not seem near yet!! These last 2 days I have had some rather exciting personal experiences, which I am not wanting every day!

Yesterday we took 2 lovely old Crusader strongholds, and strong still, I had to knock them about awfully with concentrated shellfire.

Vernon's father rode Cupid again on 16th March. He would normally have ridden his beloved Flashlight, but it was a chance to give the old boy a rest, and having the opportunity to ride either Cupid or Polly, the two other horses that had left Essex with him on 5th August 1914, was a pleasure. Vernon's father had been awarded a decoration after the first battle of Gaza and this was the day that he was to be invested in it.

Cupid was chosen, and early in the morning she had been groomed and tidied, her hooves had been oiled, her mane hogged and not a whisker left out of place. She hadn't felt so smart for at least three years.

The investiture was to take place at the Jewish Agricultural College at Tel Aviv and the decorations presented by HRH the Duke of Connaught. The whole town was in celebration, there was bunting in the streets and a band playing, and the sun was shining. Cupid much enjoyed this happy day and managed to keep looking her best, at least while she was 'on parade', and when she stood at the horse lines during the investiture; until the return journey, when as fate would have it the weather turned, black clouds rolled in, the rain fell in torrents, and the temperature plummeted. Both she and Vernon's father arrived back at Headquarters soaked to the skin and covered with mud.

His father mentions this outing in a letter written on 17th March:

Yesterday I was "invested" by the Duke of C, a very perfunctory performance, a whole lot of officers being herded into ranks, filing past HRH who pinned the medal on; the medal being subsequently removed & handed back to do duty at another investiture of another Division another day & so on. I had to ride 10 miles each way, wait 2 hours, and sign 3 army forms including a receipt for something I haven't received, all in true army fashion.

We've got cold weather again and drenching rain, everything muddy again. I am enclosing a sprig of orange blossom; the whole place smells like a wedding!

Vernon was pleased to find his horses fit and well when he returned from leave, but with great sadness he discovered that some time during March, his dog Bosche had disappeared.

During the time that the Brigade had been at Mulebbis, many stray dogs had appeared, attracted by the smells associated with an army at camp, and the chance to scavenge. They became an utter nuisance. They were flea-ridden and mangy and carried all manner of unwanted parasites and diseases. They fought amongst each other, howled through the night and were in the main very unpleasant. They were very unwelcome at the horse lines too; it would seem that horse droppings were a particular delicacy and the horses became very unsettled by them. The dogs would appear after dark causing mayhem, and the horses would kick out at them as they sniffed and scratched about under their feet. The men would chase them off with sticks and hurl stones at them, but they were brave and fearless creatures and it was hard to keep them away. The men were not keen to be too close to them either, as stray dogs in this part of the world could easily be carrying rabies and this was a risk not to be taken.

It is thought that Bosche had probably got into a fight with one of these strays and been either killed or mortally wounded; no sign of him was ever found. It was also during this time that Lordy the goose vanished, the stray dogs being the likely cause of her demise as well.

Vernon briefly mentions Bosche's disappearance in a letter he wrote on 6th April:

I am now back with the Bde. again. Fortunately they have not moved since I left and so are pretty comfortable.

The country is all looking perfectly lovely now, most luxuriant growth everywhere and all kinds of wild flowers it really is ripping, wild hyacinths, crocuses, tulips and many others. They have all been having great fun while I have been away with race meetings, football matches and boxing and concerts.

Cupid & Polly my horses are very well, but little Bosche has gone which is very sad, I have hopes that he may turn up again but he has been gone a long time.

CHAPTER THIRTEEN

Summer arrived and with it came the heat and the flies. The spring months had provided a merciful relief from them, but soon they were as bad as ever. Cupid was made to wear a fly fringe again, which she hated, as the beastly thing seemed always in the way. At least it did to some extent keep her eyes free from the torment, though the clouds of flies that would sometimes descend on the horse lines were so indescribable that nothing would keep them away. They were a constant torment for the horses and the men.

Cupid's Brigade remained in the vicinity of Mulebbis throughout the early summer of 1918, taking part in various operations, but Cupid was not to be part of these excitements; some time during July, Vernon was posted away from the Brigade and Cupid and Polly were to go with him. He was given command of a section of the Divisional Ammunition Column (DAC), whose job it was to supply the Battery positions with ammunition and other supplies as and when they were needed. The ammunition was collected from the ammunition dumps and hauled up to the Batteries on wagons; this was very hard work for the horses that pulled the wagons and for the mules that carried the bulk of the lighter equipment. The DAC could be called on day or night to keep the Batteries supplied with whatever they needed.

During the week before Cupid and Polly joined the DAC, the men who were not up at the front had kept themselves entertained by holding a large horse show, open to all. Horses were entered from most of the neighbouring units, some from the Infantry, some from the Cavalry, many from the other Artillery Brigades and so on.

At first Cupid had enjoyed the show, as it was very reminiscent of the shows that she had been entered into before the war. She had always enjoyed the jumping, and many a rosette hung on the cupboard door in the harness room at home – witness to her achievements. Sadly there was nothing to celebrate this time. The show was to end in humiliation for her and Vernon; it seemed that nothing would go quite right for them that day. Cupid, Polly and Flashlight had all been entered into various classes, and there were crowds of men at the ringside cheering and sometimes jeering at the competitors.

On the 14th August Vernon gives a brief account of the show in a letter home:

Last week we had a horse show in one of the Infantry Brigades, a great affair quite like a pre war show. We had a team of 4 horses in but unfortunately we were defeated. I also showed Dad's big chestnut in the class for chargers but they said he was lame, quite true moreover; I had no time to get his stiffness off before we went into the ring. Lastly I jumped my mare Cupid and knocked down a brick in the wall and the post and rail jump but as about 30% of the entries refused at the first fence it was not so bad.

The next thing of note that has happened of interest is that I have left the Brigade and gone to the Divisional Ammunition Column. I have about 130 men, of whom 40% are Indians and 170 mules and horses.

Life with the Ammunition Column was very busy. There were rumours in the air that an advance was to be made early in the autumn; thousands of rounds of ammunition were carried up to the front and all the equipment was made ready. As ever the wheelwrights, farriers, saddlers and blacksmiths were hard at work. Many of the wagons that had travelled with the Brigade all the way from Suez were suffering from the wear and tear of continuous use over eighteen months and were badly in need of some attention.

Thousands of troops were gathering in the area, and Cupid had never seen such sights. Every day she and Vernon would travel with the mules and the wagons carting huge loads up to depots nearer the front. It was fortunate for her that her section of the DAC was attached to her old Brigade, allowing her and Vernon to keep in contact with old friends as well as making new ones, Cupid liked the Indians. They were kind and gentle people to work with and nothing much would fluster them, which was fortunate as there was a good deal of competition between them and other users of the narrow roads and tracks along which they carried their loads.

They were expected to share the roads and other supply routes with the more modern equipment of the army in Palestine. Men in motor cars would speed along under clouds of dust honking their horns, great gun tractors would roar and squeak and belch their oily smoke, armoured cars would rattle along with a man's head protruding from the turret on top, and motorcycles delivering despatches would fly past. All of them would demand right of passage over the wagons and mules of Cupid's section. A convoy of horse-drawn ammunition wagons and a train of mules, all heavily laden, was an unwieldy thing at the best of times and these stand-offs would sometimes cause fierce arguments between the tired and frustrated men.

The rumours of the advance soon became fact. Thousands of troops had gathered in the area, ships from the Royal Navy sailed off the coast and the air was buzzing with aircraft; this was to be the offensive that finally broke the Turkish army. On 19th September at 04.30 it all began. The advance was to be made up through the coastal region between the Mediterranean and the Judean Hills, and would not stop until the Turkish armistice was signed on 31st October 1918.

CHAPTER FOURTEEN

Cupid's march north along the coast began at the end of September in the wake of the defeated Turkish army; her section of the DAC was still attached to her old Brigade and it was a long and tortuous march. The Brigade took part in some stiff fighting during the first few days of the advance and consequently Cupid's section was kept very busy resupplying them with all they needed. The Turkish army was soon overwhelmed by this massive and well-planned attack. History does not relate the exact journey that Cupid made during this first stage of the advance, but they reached Haifa on 2nd October, where they rested for three weeks.

Haifa proved to be a great rest for the horses, mainly because there was a bountiful supply of fresh water, but it was here that the men began to suffer from attacks of malaria - their march had taken them through one of the worst malarial belts - and for the first time, Spanish influenza. The epidemic of 1918 killed more people than the entire war.

The march continued on 22nd October from Haifa up the coast towards Acre, en route to Beirut. This part of the journey was to be very hard on the horses and the men; the weather was excessively hot and they were plagued by torrential thunderstorms. On top of this, rations and forage were in short supply. More men fell daily to malaria, sandfly fever or influenza.

They were marching in one vast column and Cupid's Brigade was marching with an Infantry Brigade, so you can imagine what a sizeable operation this was. When the sun shone the dust was unbearable; it choked the eyes, nose and throat. When the thunderstorms erupted everything was drenched, and the stifling heat and humidity was desperately tiring.

The guns travelled with the Brigade and Cupid and Vernon followed with their wagons and mules carrying mountains of equipment. The going along the seashore was very tough and the wretched horses struggled to pull their heavy loads through the soft sand. Craving water, they quickly lost condition and with that the will to work.

Exhausted, they reached Acre on 24th October, but it was after dark before the horses were fed and watered. Every muscle in Cupid's body ached when finally the saddle was taken off her back. She stood with her head hung low listening to the men as they erected the watering troughs and prepared the meagre forage ration; so many horses and mules needed to be fed and watered. It was to be a long and uncomfortable night.

The march continued the next day and after a short while they left the sandy beach behind them and began to climb slowly up a precipitous narrow path, sometimes barely wide enough for a wagon; this path had been cut into the cliffs centuries ago by ancient pioneers. The path zigzagged up the steep cliffs, and it was a precarious journey. On many occasions Vernon would dismount and lead Cupid. Neither of them had much of a head for heights and to look down at the waves crashing on the rocks below was not an experience that they, or indeed many of the other horses and men, took kindly to. The Indians leading the mules stepped nervously over the stony path, for one false move could end in disaster. They were marching on to Tyre, a journey of about twenty-five miles, and reached it with great relief at about four o'clock that afternoon. They made camp on high, flat ground overlooking the little port of Tyre and out to sea.

The following day, 26th October they marched on towards Sidon, this time over a hard well-made road, which took them over the Nahr el Kasimir River where they camped and the horses were watered. Vernon recalls this in a note written that day:

Oct 26. A fine morning. Got onto a topping hard road about midday, just avoided rain again, those in advance got quite wet. Camped across a river (full of fish). In crossing the river we passed out of Palestine just 1 year 7 months since we entered. Put up our troughs for watering by a ruin on the edge of the river. Found a large number of blackberries, which were very good. Lost three more men to hospital.

His father writes on 27th October 1918:

We have been marching 5 days, and have 5 days marching ahead of us. I am marching with a Brigade of Infantry & some oddments: our column is 5 miles long and as we don't represent a twentieth part of the army out here you can imagine what an unwieldy thing even a Division is when confined to one road. As the enemy is reported to have retired from Aleppo it seems ridiculous that I should deal in mystery as to where I am, and I must risk the Censor making obliterations in this letter. I am now sitting on a rocky eminence 800 yards from the sea beside a hard road which we struck yesterday at Tyre: beyond me I see Sidon jutting out into a deep blue Mediterranean: on my right front are the rocky blue mountains of Lebanon, away on my right is Mt Hermon. We have marched along precipitous ledges cut out by pioneers along the cliffs running out into the sea, called the Steppes of Tyre – white promontories known by mariners in the most ancient times. The country is lovely and interesting. We bivouacked at Acre, (where Napoleon was beaten by Sir Sydney Smith), within a few hundred yards of where Napoleon had all his Artillery. Acre is a dear little town, wonderfully fortified, it has been besieged 11 times, the walls still have canon balls sticking into them, and the old dry moats & ramparts are still littered with old guns & cannon balls lying about mixed up with dead dogs, domestic utensils & the derelict remains which are the landmarks of Turkish rule.

We had horrible heavy thunderstorms, heat & some rain for the first 3 days – much malaria (we are in the worst malaria belt), I've had 2 awful heads but am very fit now. We only get bully beef, biscuits and tea, the men have had no vegetables for 6 weeks, and it's wonderful they are not worse, but I am very short of men.

In this letter Vernon's father refers to the 'Steppes of Tyre'; actually it is better known as the 'Ladder of Tyre'. After one more day's march they reach Sidon and he continues his letter:

Oct 28th

I am now sitting in a stony wheat stubble just outside Sidon, having completed a short march: the Doctor has just returned from Sidon whither we sent him to forage, he has produced 3 eggs, 3 contortionist cucumbers & 2lbs of potatoes, which has almost exhausted the resources of the place. Sidon is a tiny place on a bump poking out into the sea; one can see the old keep & fortifications rising out of the centre of it, and around are olives, orange orchards, quite good private homes, a church (Christian I think) & the usual Sheik's Tombs. The hills behind are all terraced and bear traces of intensive cultivations of former times.

A Syrian family has just ridden past me, they have been marketing in Sidon I think. Papa on a well bred Arab mare, with a large umbrella up to keep off the sun, one child in front of him & one behind & all kinds of merchandise hanging around the saddle. Mamma on a donkey with another child behind her, and large saddle bags full of weighty looking matter, then the 'scivvy' walking behind with a large ration biscuit tin on her head. Biscuit & tea tins will long be important features of household furniture in Palestine.

The health of the troops is improving as we march north & get clear of the malarial belt. At Haifa, at the foot of Mount Carmel it was very unhealthy.

Our horses are getting thin, mobile rations are scanty, & there is no grazing.

After four more days of marching they arrived at Beirut, and it was on that same day, 31st October 1918, that peace had been declared with Turkey.

A plan had been made for the Brigade to march triumphantly through Beirut, but there seemed more of an air of confusion than celebration – every man and every animal was exhausted, and it was more a sense of relief at having survived the march than a celebration that the war with Turkey was over. Anyhow, Cupid and her section of the DAC were not to be part of this triumphal march, as the last two days for them had been agony. Vernon writes in his notes:

30th October.

Got into camp on the side of a hill at 1700 impossible to get into our usual formation but managed to scramble in somehow just before dark & got the animals off to water which was about a mile off.

Tomorrow the whole Bde. Group less the section DAC (us) are to march triumphantly through the town to our destination when we hope to get a few days rest. We are to draw the Bde. rations & forage which means emptying wagons etc. and go by a short cut to our camp. Up till 2300 making arrangements. Another bad day.

31st October.

Everyone had a very disturbed night, infantry camels and shouting natives floundering in our lines all night.

Saw the Bde. off on their great march. We then followed by the aforementioned shortcut to our camp. Quite a nice camp, fairly dirty but not too bad. Planted mess by the one and only tree. Water for animals in the river.

News in the evening that an armistice had been arranged with Turkey from midday.

Capt.——- of C Battery very kindly got us some canteen stores, so drowned our sorrows in whisky and bottled Bass very glad to be at the end of our travels at last. The longest continuous march we have ever done.

That night, Cupid, Flashlight and Polly stood by the river some distance outside Beirut. They were most probably on the banks of the Beirut River, and had drunk their fill from the flowing fresh water. They were surrounded by hundreds of other horses and mules that had been led to water and many of the animals stood belly deep in the water. The whole atmosphere seemed somewhat surreal, the men apparently having left them to their own devices.

Cupid watched. There were groups of men everywhere, some sitting and chatting, some lying asleep and some singing songs. It was as if they were at home, unbridled by the disciplines of army life. Later on, Vernon came down to the river, puffing on his pipe. He threw his arms around Cupid's neck, and she could smell the alcohol on his breath. He spoke to her gently and the tears streamed down his cheeks.

It was four years, two months and twenty-seven days since Cupid had left her comfortable Essex stable. She had travelled nearly four and a half thousand miles and seen many things that she wished never to see again. What would be her future?

CHAPTER FIFTEEN

The following morning discipline was restored. Horse lines were erected and racks built on which to hang the vast quantities of harness. The wagons were put in lines and the guns smartly dressed in the gun park. Everything was cleaned and repaired and the horses groomed.

Peace had been declared with Turkey, but the war was not over – and would not be until peace was declared with Germany. As Cupid stood at the horse lines, she could hear the men deep in conversation. They none of them knew their future and they couldn't help but wonder whether if over the next weeks or months they would be sent back to the muddy horrors of the Western Front, to spend another winter in the place where they had begun their foreign service three years before.

Life became more settled over the next few days. Mercifully for the horses they were near to the river, which meant that there was always water, but there was no grazing and forage rations were very limited. It was a relief for them that there was no real work to do, as they had lost so much condition during the long march to Beirut that any hard pulling or riding would have been a real risk. Some of the poor creatures were so thin that the effort could have been fatal. It was hoped that the forthcoming rains might produce some grazing; otherwise life would become a whole lot tougher.

On 2nd November 1918 Vernon's father writes:

Two days ago we marched into BEIRUT, where we heard that peace had been declared with Turkey, thus our Palestine campaign is ended. We are camped 4 miles outside Beirut, on stony ground, surrounded by beautiful mountains, with the bay of blue sea & the red roofs & orange groves below us, a truly beautiful spot. What will happen to us is of course merest speculation.

I expect that our mail service here will be very bad, for we have no road or rail behind us, our line of communication is by sea to Port Said only, and we are at the mercy of the navy, the most autocratic institution, next to the Prussian Army, in existence. At present we are being fed on bully beef, half ration of bread, tea, onions and cheese, no milk or sugar, and a dead horse was found this morning in our drinking water supply, which of course the M.O. didn't detect in his analysis, but it tasted quite nice.

The canteen has arrived here, and I have ordered 600 bottles of beer to be issued at my expense to my Brigade & section D.A.C. on Nov 15 on which day I have commanded the Bde. 4 years, and on that day 3 years ago we went overseas to France.

At last it seems that there was something to celebrate and no doubt the beer was much enjoyed - that is if the autocratic Navy, which supplied the canteen, came up with the goods on the right day!

The men needed something to celebrate. They were tired and very hungry, disease was still rife among all ranks and their weak condition made things even worse. Dysentery, malaria, pneumonia and of course the Spanish influenza were seriously taking their toll.

There was also some slightly more cheery news which quickly spread through the camp; after peace had been declared with Turkey, Bulgaria and Austria had also surrendered. Surely now it was only a matter of time before Germany followed suit and the war would finally be over?

Vernon's father writes again on 7th November 1918:

Bulgaria, Turkey & Austria having surrendered it seems only a question of weeks before Germany will have to do ditto. Here we are struggling with sickness, which is bad. Very tired troops, enervated by 3 years campaigning in a hot climate, after a long march through a most unhealthy belt of country, without the bracing excitement of fighting, are an easy prey to malaria & all the fevers which we used to call "low fever". We are I hope through the worst of it and that the coming rains & cold weather will much improve matters. We are still on bully beef, and the feeding of the Division right up here is a great strain on our communications, which are by sea only. Forage for the innumerable horses, mules and camels of a mobile army is an awful business, shiploads are consumed daily, & the horses are as thin as rakes after they've eaten it. It is trying to rain, & still very hot, with violent storms of wind: when the rain comes we shall have some grazing I hope. We have no letters or newspapers from home after 1st Oct, and bar the official communiqués we know nothing. But if ever one should have patience and not grumble it is now.

Over the next day or two, the weather began to change; the rain that had started as not much more than humid air began to fall in torrents, the heat and humidity vanished and the temperature plummeted. The river became swollen and it became much more difficult to water the horses, as so many hundreds of horses and mules needed to be taken to water. The operation became staggered and continued all day every day; that and a continuous stream of wagons bringing forage up from the docks was a full time job, and it was a job that Cupid and her section DAC were fully employed at. Every day Vernon would ride her or Polly back and forth to the dockside with the convoys of wagons overloaded with piles of valuable feed. One day, Vernon's father came with them, for what reason is unknown, but his outing ended in rather an undignified manner. He mentions it briefly in one of his letters:

Old Flashlight gave me such a roll yesterday, I was riding him with a fly fringe on his brow band (which I never do) and he fell into a ditch which he didn't see, & though he rolled about on me & I had a leg hung up in the stirrup he, as the real gentleman he is didn't hurt me a scrap.

Perhaps all that was hurt was his pride, but for certain this unfortunate episode will have caused much mirth amongst the men, seeing their Commanding Officer rolling about in a muddy ditch.

Thankfully the rains began to produce a little grazing, which eased the pressure, but it was to take time before the horses really began to benefit from it. Everything that grew was eaten before it had a chance to be of any real use and, because when the rains started they fell in such torrents, the whole place soon became a quagmire of mud, more like Flanders than Beirut. These conditions did nothing to improve the lives of the horses or the morale of the men.

Beirut on Monday 11th November 1918 was cold and wet. Cupid and Polly had been back and forth to the docks three times that day; Polly had been lent to another man who was roped in to help bring the convoys of rations up from the ships. So many of the horses were in a state of exhaustion that any sound animal was having to double its workload, and the sickness amongst the men was such that any spare hands were immediately put to use.

The day dragged on and by the evening when the saddles had at last been taken from their backs and they were standing worn out at the horse lines, eating their meagre rations from a nose-bag, having earlier been watered by Vernon and his companion, who had ridden them into the flooded river after delivering the final load of forage of the day. Every muscle in Cupid's lean body ached, and she wondered if she would ever stand in a warm, dry stable again with a bed of deep straw, well fed and groomed after a long day's hunting, listening to the wind outside, content and happy.

That evening as the light began to fade, suddenly a great crescendo of noise erupted. Ships' hooters from the Bay of St George outside the harbour boomed out, bells began to ring and the men began to shout and sing. Up on the hills fires were lit and all sense of army discipline seemed to vanish – news had arrived that an armistice had been signed with Germany at five o'clock that morning and all hostilities were to cease at 11 am.

The sense of celebration was overwhelming.

It seemed to Cupid that in a matter of minutes the world had gone crazy. The men who were at the horse lines stopped their work, and many of the horses were just left to roam about. The men embraced each other, they embraced the horses, they danced jigs and sang songs. Guns began to fire and a band played. Very lights lit up the sky and rockets whistled through the air. It was an extraordinary scene and the celebrations were to last all night.

Vernon's father wrote on 12th November 1918:

Yesterday evening we heard that peace had been declared, or rather an armistice with Germany, which is the same thing. So we mobilised the Divisional Band, sang God Save the King, & I fired a Royal Salute of 21 guns from my Howitzers, which resulted in only 21 puffs of burning cordite; there was a great tolling of bells from all the Christian churches, much firing of very lights and rockets, and as much "booze" as campaigning circumstances permit. It is hard to realise that it is all over, and I confess that my feelings rushed home to imagine the deep thankfulness that must have come over England, the weight lifted off every house, the feelings of genuine national pride in having been stout hearted enough to have seen it through, and the realisation that no sacrifices have been wasted. If ever I were proud of my country it is now, the grit & guts are there as ever.

Vernon came to the horse lines, climbed onto Cupid's back and rode her bareback down to watch the guns firing their salute; it was a better view from her back. Both he and Cupid seemed to have forgotten that it was raining and cold. Quite where the "booze" came from is a bit of a mystery, but safe to say there was enough to go around.

It wasn't until the next morning that the true state of affairs became a reality. There was nothing the men could do to improve the lives of the horses. They lived at the horse lines, standing in the drenching rain, hock deep in mud; they were still on half rations and other than the animals used to ferry the supplies up from the dockside, there was no work for them and no exercise to warm them. The guns stood silent in the gun-parks and more and more men succumbed to disease; the celebrations were soon forgotten and the future looked bleak.

Vernon's father continues his letter:

It is streaming with rain and bitterly cold: I am not at all looking forward to a 150 mile march, sleeping every night on wet mud and possibly getting bogged, about 50% below strength & none of the men strong at that.

My camp and bivouacs are in an awful mess, one carries a ton of weight on ones boots & the horses are standing in water. One feels marooned up here, no roads or railway to the base, a rotten little harbour which makes it almost impossible to ship horses and guns from here. They will not I am sure ship any of these horses home, if they get them to Egypt they'll turn them into hides and tallow, if we leave them here we will have to shoot the lot.

Well my dear, so ends the Great War, it is something to think about rather than talk about, it is too big a thing to write about, there is no appropriate language.

The Great War was over, but other than that one night of carefree celebration, the morale of the men was at a very low state. Their thoughts were of home and their families, but the prospects of getting there were virtually nil. It seemed certain that they wouldn't be going home from Beirut, and the prospect of marching some or all of the way back to Egypt also seemed impossible. The poor health of the men and the horses, combined with the weather, added to the sense of gloom.

As the days went on they became more used to their surroundings. Cupid and Vernon were kept busy with the endless ferrying of supplies. As they traipsed back and forth from the harbour they came more and more into contact with the local population and were shocked by what they saw; the war had deprived them of almost everything – starving children begged for food and their mothers begged for blankets or any cast-off clothes. Many of them were half naked, and it was a shocking sight to see.

In one of his letters Vernon remarks:

The poor people all round are in a most parlous condition they come round our camps and pick out the rubbish for food and they have hardly any clothes on. They say that in the province of Lebanon alone 250,000 people have died of starvation since the war, & I'm afraid local appearances justify this statement.

Our poor men and horses and mules have such a rotten time when it rains, there is no chance of getting any billets for them at present. Cupid and Polly are well, Cupid is fatter and I hope that if any horses are taken home that they will take her. Polly has not been so well and looks very old now, I am afraid they would not think her worth taking.

His father writes again on 14th November:

We are in a proper muddle here, as bad a crisis to deal with as any unfortunate battle. It has rained in torrents for 3 days, my camps & bivouacs are as bad as Flanders, the men are going down like ninepins, we are under half effective strength, and we have orders to march to Ludd, which is 200 miles of which 150 is roadless. It is impossible, we cannot even start; we should lose men & horses (& eventually guns) all along the route. I cannot contemplate the pitiable remnant that would reach Ludd. The fact is the men are low in vitality, and this epidemic produces alarming results. Epidemics occur in populations that are poorly fed, poorly housed & low in vitality. The Cavalry, Horse Artillery and Infantry are if anything worse off than we are for some have been in a worse malarious district and had even less medical facilities. As well as malaria we have had what they call Spanish Influenza, but all these things have the same symptoms, high fever & subsequent debility. I am getting some of my men into buildings of sorts but buildings in this dirty country are liable to harbour typhus lice and other suchlike domestic animals.

This reads rather alarmingly! & a poor sequel to peace, & I don't know why I should write it except that it relieves me, and it is war history. I am right down sorry for my men who are now marooned, sick, overworked, underfed, far from home and for all they know to the country clean forgotten.

The last three weeks of November 1918 were as tough as any that the men and their horses had suffered throughout the war, apart from actual fighting; the men did their best for the horses, as they had always done, but it was a daily struggle, such were the shortages of food and veterinary supplies and the desperately unhealthy conditions in which they were living.

These are best described in the letters written home.

On 17th November Vernon's father writes:

Today is fine and we are drying, I have moved one Battery into warehouses, & one on the sea shore is on dry sand & has a sort of empty barn & as many tents as I can give it, those men will be dry too. The third Battery was so reduced by sickness until it had no officers left and only 50 men out of 140 that I have split it up, and attached one half of the remnants to A Btty & the other half to B Btty. My Adjt. & Orderly Officer are both sick; on my HdQtrs my Sgt. Major & Corporal are both in Hospital. The Infantry Battalions are down to about 250 each instead of 700 or 800, and we are waiting for orders to march 200 miles of which 150 are road-less, over clay & cotton soil, the heaviest imaginable. They send us no reinforcements, the send us incomplete rations, we have run out of Veterinary stores, horses die of colic, the medical services are chaotic, & Commanding Officers are bubbling over with fury – fury directed at the old object, the Mandarins who don't have to handle men, who don't live in "bivvies" in the mud, who don't have to take 8 mules to water twice a day in the streaming rain, who live up aloft in beautiful clothes, and who have never read the first page of the Staff Manual.

Anyway I am feeling much happier now that I have got all my men some shelter from the elements. If we have to march I shall send all the weaklings into hospital at once, & with the fit we will do our best, but I quite expect to have to jettison along the route first my ammunition (which they say we must carry because it is unboxed, while the ration

ships daily return empty) then my wagons then my guns then the supply
wagons & do the last lap on any poor old hairies that can carry us!

If we march you will have a gap in letters, I shall certainly not be
able to write for about 16 days.

The state of this country is pitiful, my experiences of going round
looking for billeting accommodation gave me an insight into the life of
the people here. In one house, a house of the people usually a square
box of one or sometimes 2 rooms with wooden shutters, a flat roof,
iron bars to windows, & made of large blocks of stone, no glass to
windows, no furniture, cement or mud floor, I found a dead child, a
little girl, just lying on her quilt, she'd been dead any number of months,
no one had taken the slightest notice. In another I found a boy dying
& a poor mother whisking the flies off him, no furniture no food no
vessels of any sort in the house. In quite a good house I found a dying
man in one room & a dying woman in another, helpless to each other,
just skeletons with some transparent skin over them. A dead figure at
the side of the road excites no wonder. In this way three quarters of the
population of Lebanon have disappeared in 4 years.

The rains continued and it soon became clear that marching,
even for some of the way, back to Egypt was an impossibility; there
were no roads, no lines of communication and the poor state of
health of the men and the wretched horses that would have to
carry them or haul the mountains of equipment finally put an end
to this ridiculous plan.

It was the whole Division, of which Cupid's Brigade was part, that
had to be shipped back to Egypt. Eventually embarkation orders
were received and the slow process began on 28th November.

Finally on the 12th December 1918 Cupid, Polly and Flashlight found themselves back on board a ship; the sun was shining as the SS *Huntsgreen* eased her way out of Beirut harbour. The ship took them to Kantara and following a short railway journey they arrived back in Cairo on 14th December.

Their new camp was at a place called Helmeih, close to Heliopolis. The camp was on sand and it was dry, the sky was blue and the sun shone.

The six weeks that they had spent at Beirut had taken their toll. Many horses had died and some of the weaker ones had been destroyed, considered too weak to make the journey. Worst of all, a good many of the stronger horses had been left as re-mounts for the troops that were left behind – a huge wrench for the men who had looked after them and nurtured them for so long.

For the lucky ones their new camp was a luxury in comparison; the horse lines were dry, the weather was good and most importantly, there was a plentiful supply of food and water.

Over the next few days the men spent much time with the horses. They were clipped, groomed, reshod and made to look as smart as possible, smarter perhaps than they had looked since leaving England over three years before. Vernon was determined that Cupid should look at her very best. He spent hours with her, talking to her gently as he groomed her, reminiscing about the things that they had done and the sights they had seen. He was relaxed and more importantly, so was she – she couldn't remember when she had last felt so good.

On the evening of 19th December Vernon's father inspected the Brigade. Nothing had been left untouched, the guns gleamed, all the harness was polished and the brasses twinkled in the late sunshine. It was a very pleasing sight.

At first light the following morning the whole Division began to wind its way out of the camp. The Divisional band was playing and crowds lined the streets and cheered them as they passed. It was to be a day of great celebration concluding with a ceremonial march past General Sir Edmund Allenby at Opera Square, Cairo.

His father rode Flashlight, Vernon rode Cupid and another man rode Polly; the three old stable-mates from Essex could not have been more proud.

They returned to the camp at Helmeih that evening, and after the horses were 'put to bed' and made as comfortable as possible, a huge Christmas party was held. Cupid stood content at the horse lines listening to the bands playing and the men singing; it was truly peace at last.

CHAPTER SIXTEEN

The Christmas party at Helmieh was the last time that Cupid's Brigade was together as one unit. Over the next few days, including Christmas Day, men started to leave in batches to be repatriated and demobilised; they would go to the embarkation camp at Kantara to await the ships that would take them home. The usual journey would be by ship to Taranto, Italy, and then by rail through Italy and France, a journey of about two weeks.

Vernon's turn came soon in the new year; during the first few days of January 1919 he rode Cupid every day. He knew that he would have to leave her, but had hopes that it might still be possible to get her home. On 14th January 1919 he writes:

I must write and warn you that I am on my way home to be demobilised, and it is only fair that you should be prepared for such a distressing situation!!!

They have decided to demobilise all students etc. At present we have got as far as Taranto having left Egypt on the 6th. Tomorrow we embark on the train and should be in England in about 10 days, we then go to camp and get properly demobilised.

I have had to leave my horses at Cairo but we have faint hopes that we may be able to get one home, Dad is going to have a try before he comes.

More and more men departed over the next few weeks and there were often fond farewells made between the men and their horses; many of the horses like Cupid, Polly and Flashlight had survived the entire war and the bond between them and the men was very strong. Had they had a choice the men would have brought all of them home and back to the lives that had been wrenched from them some four and a half years before. These gallant horses now faced an uncertain future and as time went on it seemed less and less likely that any would be taken home, which made the parting even more difficult.

For the horses themselves, life at Helmeih was not at all bad; the men looked after them well - they hadn't a lot else to do while they waited for their turn to leave for home - food was plentiful and the horses soon put on weight for the first time in months. Regular exercise was given in the form of competition. Jumping and racing became a daily routine, and some of the horses were even tried at playing polo.

Vernon's father tried and kept trying to find a way of getting Cupid home, but as time went by this seemed less and less likely. In February 1919, the Government decided that none of the horses from Egypt would be brought home. He writes to his son on 16th February 1919:

We sent home about 2000 [men] from the Division last week, and about 1500 a week are to go. Our Brigade has done very well in Athletic Sports, but we were beaten first tier in football. It is getting hot and dusty and boring past description. No horses at all are to be taken home from Egypt, all our 15 to be destroyed & the younger ones for Army of Occupation. I occasionally ride your mares, who are very fat & sleek on unlimited food.

Cupid and Polly lived side by side for all the time they were at Helmeih and Flashlight too would sometimes join them, though as the absolute favourite of Vernon's father he would at most times be living nearer to Brigade Headquarters and enjoying a rather more 'First Class' existence.

During the night of 20 – 21st February 1919 a hot wind blew over the camp at Helmeih, not quite severe enough to cause a sandstorm but enough to cause some damage to the horse lines and to blow things about. Men spent most of the night retrieving equipment that had been blown about the place. They wanted to be asleep and were annoyed at this inconvenience. Strange that such a small event could cause such annoyance considering what most of them had witnessed over the past four and a half years, but they had had enough. Many of their friends were already at home with their families, and this was all they wanted.

The horses and mules were unsettled; a small group of mules broke loose from their enclosure, a sort of sandy paddock fenced with hurdles. One of the hurdles had collapsed when the restless creatures had pushed against it. The escapees began to charge about the camp; the disgruntled men began to chase them, cursing and swearing at yet more disruption to their sleep.

One of the mules charged through the horse lines, causing chaos. It bit and kicked its way down the line. Cupid was in the middle of this path of destruction and as the mule came alongside her she felt a surging burst of pain and collapsed to the floor.

It was now beginning to get light. The wind had dropped a little, but sand and dust still swirled about. Cupid was lying on the sand. She no longer felt in any pain. She tried to get up, but her legs refused to work.

She felt someone stroking her ears and heard a gentle voice talking to her. Two or three other men were kneeling beside her – she recognised the voice of Vernon's father and felt completely at peace as she listened to his gentle comforting voice. She closed her eyes and suddenly she was back in Essex, Vernon was on her back, hounds in full cry. She felt the east wind on her face as they galloped on towards a five-bar gate which they flew over, and there she was back in her own field on the farm that she had left four years and seven months before. It was her heaven.

On 24th February Vernon's father writes to his son:

I have been sitting in my tent today in a Khamsin wind writing letters. I have bad news to tell you, for I have had to destroy poor old Cupid; she had a frightful set to with a wandering mule at night, was horribly mauled, in fact I am not sure she hadn't a broken leg. She didn't suffer long; we had 3 vets, & decided to shoot her. I have told the Vet Sergt. to keep & clean out a shoe for you. She was a quarrelsome little devil on the lines always, & wherever she stood she managed to have a row with a neighbour or a loose horse.

Govt. will send no horses home, poor old Polly will have to be destroyed, but not till I go, she is fat and lazy on heaps of food. I have had her marked D (for destruction). I hate this part of war, but I know it is inevitable.

EPILOGUE

Vernon would have been deeply saddened to receive this letter. He had been determined, despite any Government rules or regulations, to do all he could to get Cupid home. Whether he would have succeeded or not, of course we will never know.

The Veterinary Sergeant did however clean out and keep one of Cupid's hoofs. This may sound slightly morbid to some, but it was brought home by Vernon's father and made into a doorstop as a permanent memory of the little horse.

On the day he gave me the book, my grandfather also showed me the doorstop and told me about Cupid. Even then, all those years later, he wished that he could have brought her home.

He had a lifelong love of horses and was still riding when he was over eighty; he went hunting on his eightieth birthday. Throughout his life he owned many horses, but he never forgot his first, his fifteenth birthday present.

He died in 1981, just short of his eighty-fifth birthday.